INDIA'S WOMEN SCIENTISTS

By the Same Author

Operation Polo

Kakori

Ganesha's Global Startup

Startup Secrets from the Ramayana

The Legends of a Startup Guy

Super Siblings

Super Couples

Super Women

INDIA'S WOMEN SCIENTISTS

PRACHI GARG

An imprint of
Srishti Publishers & Distributors

Srishti Publishers & Distributors
A unit of AJR Publishing LLP
212A, Peacock Lane
Shahpur Jat, New Delhi – 110 049

editorial@srishtipublishers.com

First published by Bold,
An imprint of Srishti Publishers & Distributors in 2026

10 9 8 7 6 5 4 3 2 1

This is a work of non-fiction based on the author's research about the subject. While due care has been taken by the author and publisher to verify contents at press time, any inadvertent miss that is brought to their notice shall be duly verified and updated subsequently. Actual names of people and places have been used with a view to provide firsthand information.

Printed and bound in India

This book is dedicated to women
whose brilliance broke glass ceilings,
expanding science's horizons
for generations daring to dream.

Contents

Acknowledgements

This book has been possible due to the enormous love and support that people have given me. Their constant encouragement kept me going and ensured that I could deliver it on time. I extend my heartfelt thanks to everyone who made this journey smooth and meaningful.

Family plays a pivotal role in making such accomplishments possible, and in my case, this couldn't be truer. Each one of them has been instrumental and present whenever I needed them. My special gratitude to my father, Brijesh Garg, and my mother, Neeru Garg, for their unwavering belief in me. A warm thank you to my siblings, whose presence, humour, and steady support have been a constant source of strength.

My sincere appreciation to Mr Arup Bose from Srishti Publishers for believing in my concept and agreeing to publish the book. A heartfelt thanks to my editors, whose patience, keen eye, and thoughtful suggestions refined the manuscript beautifully. I am also grateful to the entire Srishti team for their dedication, coordination, and seamless efforts in bringing this book to life.

My deepest thanks to all my friends who provided unwavering moral support throughout this journey.

To the readers of *Kakori, Superwomen, SuperCouples, Supersiblings, The Legends of a Startup Guy, Startup Secrets from the Ramayana,* and *Ganesha's Global Startup*—your love and encouragement have inspired me to pursue new ideas.

And finally, a very special mention to my furry babies, whose unconditional love, joyful chaos, and comforting presence lifted my spirits on the most challenging days. They kept me grounded, motivated, and surrounded with warmth every single step of the way.

1.

Anandibai Gopalrao Joshi

Anandibai Gopalrao Joshi was the first Indian female doctor of Western Medicine. She was the first woman from India (under British rule) to study and graduate with a two-year degree in Western Medicine from the United States.

It is not easy for women in this era of work. So, a hundred-plus years ago, it was unimaginably difficult for women to even think about going out and making a life for themselves. Despite all that, some women went off the set path and chose to do things that not only mattered to them, but also mattered to society as well. One such woman was Anandibai Gopalrao Joshi.

Anandibai Gopalrao Joshi was a trendsetter who became the first female Indian physician. She has left a rich legacy in the field of medicine that motivated many Indian women and inspired them to study and pursue their dreams. Even for Anandi Gopalrao, the aspiration did not start from childhood. She had a very regular upbringing, like any girl in those times, but fortunately, things changed for her after marriage. She suffered the loss of her newborn baby, which led her to pursue medicine because she had experienced the lack of medical facilities.

Anandibai was not even born with that name. In those days, women changed their names after marriage. She was born as Yamuna on 31 March 1865 in then Poonah, Maharashtra. Typical of any Chitpavan Brahmin lineage, she came from a rich landlord family who paid heavy taxes to the British. Her father, Gunputrao Amritaswar Joshee and mother, Gungabai Joshee, were supportive of her homeschooling.

Anandibai was the sixth of ten children in a large family with a lot of gender discrimination. Of her four brothers, two died, and of the five sisters, the first and the fourth died soon after birth. In those days, infant mortality was high. Little did Anandibai know that she, too, would experience some of this pain. At the age of nine, a very suitable match in the form of Gopalrao Joshi came her way. He was almost 20 years older than her, but because of a good match and the desire to wed off a girl early in life, Yamuna had to settle in matrimony without completing her schooling or having any aspirations for a career.

Gopalrao was a clerk in the small city of Kayan in the Thane district of Maharashtra. Like all Marathi families, Yamuna too dropped her maiden name and was now called Anandibai, which meant "Joy of my Heart". Anandibai had not experienced any particular hardships as her father's family was well-to-do. However, Gopalrao was an honest man, and his salary was just about enough to meet their modest needs. At a very young age, she began to do household chores and carry out the responsibilities of the house. Both husband and wife were simple-hearted people who had found a supportive partnership in marriage. However, Gopalrao wanted Anandibai to be educated and would be fiercely angry on seeing her preoccupied with household chores. He proactively encouraged her to study and even tried enrolling her in school so she could get a formal education. In many ways, he was opposed to the societal trends and the opposite of many other men who were far from encouraging women to study.

In 1878, at just the age of fourteen, Anandibai gave birth to a son. However, this happiness was temporary as the baby lived only for 10 days before succumbing to death because of an illness. This left a big imprint on her mind as she realized the importance of medical life support. She said to Gopalrao, "A child's death does no harm to its father, but its mother does not want it to die." Gopalrao could see that his wife's agony needed to find the right and constructive flow to solve the bigger issues of the world.

He was a progressive thinker and an educated person. He wanted Anandibai to pursue higher studies in medicine. He made it his mission to push Anandibai on this journey. Once he saw her working in the kitchen, he was immensely furious at her for ignoring her studies. He even revolted against his mother, who made a strong case for a daughter-in-law helping in household chores. Gopalrao started finding ways through which she could pursue her education. Through several consultations and inputs from well-wishers, he finally decided to send Anandibai to America to pursue a course in medicine. However, he knew that it would be difficult and expensive for them.

On 4 September 1878, he wrote a letter addressed to the Presbyterian missionaries explaining the plight of Anandibai and how her pursuit of medicine would be a blessing for several in India. He wrote to Dr Royal Wilder, a well-known American missionary. In the letter, he stressed her interest in studying in the US and asked about any suitable posts for himself as well.

The letter was forwarded to the 'Missionary Review' and was finally published in the Princeton Missionary Review. In the letter, Gopal also expressed that he would even be willing to live in America if his wife could study there. Dr Wilder published the letter in his review so that he could also publish his response to Gopalrao's letter. Dr Wilder discouraged the proposal mainly because he did not wish for any unconverted Hindu to come to America. But the correspondence in the public domain turned opposite to what he had thought.

In the meantime, destiny had other plans for them. This letter from Gopalrao reached a resident of Roselle in New Jersey. Mrs Theodicia Carpentra was an empathetic and well-read lady. Once, she was waiting for her dentist's appointment when she came across this letter and got interested. Mrs Carpentra, herself, was remarkable in philosophy and spirituality. She identified with Anandibai's portrait in the letter. She made a note of the address and thought of responding to Gopalrao's request.

Mrs Carpenter gave a lot of thought to Anandibai and Gopalrao's request for studies. While she knew very little about British India, she felt sympathetic to the request that came from such a suppressed setting for women. She wrote back, responding to the request for higher studies and any role that Anandibai could play. Mrs Carpenter offered a lot of support and encouragement in her letter.

This letter and assurance were a big support for Anandibai. For the first time, she felt confident about being able to pursue her dream of studying medicine. Soon after receiving the first letter, she spoke to Gopalrao. He was very pleased to see that Anandibai had found a connection in the letter. He encouraged her to reply and share her thinking and plans with Mrs Carpenter.

Then began a series of exchanges between Anandibai and Mrs Carpenter. For Mrs Carpenter, the letters from Anandibai covered varied subjects about the culture and setting in India, Hindu manners and customs, and everything else that was happening in British India. For Anandibai, the letters had answers to all her queries about the possible options to pursue, the setup that she would have to adopt, and what could be the potential next steps for her to study. They also exchanged photographs, newspaper articles, magazines, and even flowers and seeds. These letters became so much more than just a means of communication for both of them. They got a peek into each other's lives and countries, which were very different, and hence both got curious about the other side of the world. What impressed Mrs Carpenter the most about the letters and Anandibai was that, despite all the drawbacks in her setting, her English was very elegant and polished.

Eventually, Gopalrao and Anandibai moved to Calcutta because of Gopalrao's work. The culture and ways of living in Calcutta were very different from those in Maharashtra. Everything was different for the couple, and it was not easy for them to settle. They were both frustrated with the challenges. Anandibai experienced discrimination as the people of Calcutta always judged and gossiped about her appearance, leaving her feeling isolated.

One of the other bigger concerns for Anandibai was the recurring headaches and fever that she had been experiencing for a long time. It had all started a year back, before they moved to Calcutta and had worsened over time. She was not even able to do her regular chores and was heavily dependent on friends for help. She had to be left at someone's house while Gopalrao was out for work. Anandibai felt frustrated and helpless in these situations. She continued to discuss the hardships of her life with Mrs Carpenter.

On hearing about Anandibai's illness, Mrs Carpenter realized that she was seriously ill. Mrs Carpenter got a doctor to prescribe medicines for her and started sending them to her along with the letters. Anandibai received the medicines and took them for the next few months. Her situation improved, but it was only temporary. Little did she know that eventually this situation would get much more serious. She expressed her gratitude to Mrs Carpenter for sending the medicines that helped her.

In due course, Gopalrao was moved from Calcutta to Serampore. This was a much smaller town in the Hubli district of West Bengal. Financially, things were not working well for the couple. Gopalrao was still very determined to send Anandibai to America. They continued to discuss and deliberate on the possible routes and costs of travel. On one such occasion, Gopalrao suggested that Anandibai travel alone. Initially, all this was very shocking for Anandibai, but she was convinced that this meant, she had to pursue bigger goals for the country.

Many European friends encouraged her to study abroad. But their families were not happy about the fact that she would travel alone, leaving her husband behind. During all this, Gopalrao continued to be supportive and kept reminding her about the goal that the couple had set for themselves. While all this was going on, they came across Dr and Mrs Thorborn in Serampore. On hearing about their desire to study medicine, the Thorborns suggested applying to the Women's Medical College of Pennsylvania. Mrs Thorborn herself had graduated from the college and suggested that it would be well-suited for Anandibai's plans for higher studies. Dr Thorborn wrote to the College in Philadelphia asking for admission. After a few weeks, Gopalrao received a letter from Dr Thorborn stating that the college had accepted Anandibai for the medicine course. Anandibai was ecstatic about this opportunity. She could see that, finally, her husband's and her dream of pursuing further studies was going to become a reality.

Dr Thorborn told Gopalrao that a party of ladies by the 'City of Calcutta' was planning to travel later in the year. This would be safe for young women to travel. This would also carry other students of Philadelphia. Anandibai started her preparations to travel. As Gopalrao worked in the post office and they lived in the post-office building, often the building was surrounded by groups of Bengalis from all castes. There was very little societal acceptance of their plans, and people looked down on the couple.

Gopalrao was a very principled person and believed that nothing wrong was being done by him and his wife. He discussed the issue with Anandibai and advised her to speak about her travel in the College Hall.

On 24 February 1883, Anandibai addressed a big crowd in the college. Till that date, no woman, not even a European, had addressed the public. Anandibai had not made any special preparations for the talk. She was nervous about her first public speech, and that too in a language that she did not speak regularly. However, her command and confidence in the room were remarkable. Her topic of speech was 'My future visit to America and public inquiries regarding it.' She categorically laid out some questions.

She started by addressing that women, be it of any origin, are averse to exposing themselves in case of a health emergency or treatments to doctors of the other sex. This meant that many women went without any medical health service providers. So, wasn't it the duty of everyone to solve this problem? It is for this cause that she was going to America. As a result of this speech, many people in the audience and many people who were not able to make it sent letters of support, appreciation, and financial aid to Anandibai and Gopalrao.

Finally, after much planning and rescheduling, Anandibai was able to travel to America on 7 April 1883. She travelled with a group of ladies, which included Mrs Thorborn and reached New York on 4 June 1883. On reaching America, she was received by Mrs Carpenter. Through years of exchanges over letters, she had already made a place for them in her heart.

Anandibai knew that she was in a foreign land and was worried about being dreary or vulgar because she did not have manners. Instead, her story and curiosity got many strangers interested and supportive of her dream. She stayed with Mr and Mrs Carpenter for some time and shared her experience of staying in America. She was finally away from the bitterness and the dissatisfied folks who had always questioned her goals. Even though Anandibai was far from her country and community, she knew that she had to be focused on the goals she had travelled for.

As things progressed, Anandbai received a scholarship for a short course in another college in New York, but she carefully assessed and discussed the same with her friends. She decided that it was best that she do the full course at the Women's Medical College of Pennsylvania.

Anandibai wrote to Rachel Bodley, the dean of the college, requesting admission. Her admission was gladly accepted as the dean was very impressed with her at first sight. It was not only because of the motivation with which she came but also because of the curiosity that was inherent in her. While there were a few other international students as well, Anandibai was the only one who wore her traditional dress. Dr Bodley was very impressed with Anandibai and her confidence in her culture and tradition.

Unfortunately, while Anandibai was studying, her health deteriorated, and she remained sick because of the cold weather. She came down with diphtheria and got some medical attention from a trained nurse. Though her health did not stabilize, she continued to work hard to complete the course. She then contracted tuberculosis, and things were not looking good for her. Gopalrao Joshi was very concerned about his wife's health. Little did he know that Dr Bodley was taking extremely good care of her.

In the summer of 1886, her plans suddenly changed when Dr Bodley learned about a resident physician in the new Albert Edward Hospital in Kolhapur, where Anandibai applied. She finally graduated with an MD in 1886 and eventually accepted and planned to return to India. Her topic of the thesis was 'Obstetric among the Aryan Hindus'. She studied both Western Medicine and Ayurvedic texts for her thesis. She finally returned to India in October 1886 and received a grand welcome back for everything that she had achieved. All of her family came to Bombay to receive her. She returned to Kolhapur and temporarily took on the role; however, her health deteriorated immensely. Her doctors did not allow her to travel and advised her to rest. Ultimately, she was allowed to go back to Poonah, the place where she had spent a lot of her childhood. Unfortunately, her health was not on track for recovery, and she died of tuberculosis on 26 February 1887 in Poonah (now Pune).

Her life story has been written about and screened. An American writer wrote her biography, and a Hindi series was broadcast on her life in India. There was recognition for her work when the Government of Maharashtra rolled out a fellowship in her name for young women working on women's health. She became the first Indian woman who, in spite of several hardships, continued to pursue her dream in the field of medicine just so that she could be of service to India. Anandibai influenced many lives and continues to do so till date.

2.

Janaki Ammal

Janaki Ammal was India's first female botanist who did path-breaking work in Plant Breeding, especially for Sugarcane and Brinjal.

Indian society was not supportive of women's growth and learning in any sphere of life. Education was a far-fetched dream for many. It was a rare privilege that came with only a very few households and girls who had progressive and supportive setups. One such house was that of Janaki Ammal. She did phenomenal work for botany research and development in India.

Janaki was born as the tenth child in a blended family of 19 brothers and sisters in the small town of Thalassery in Kerala. She grew up in a society where education for girls was not common. However, her father, Dewan Bahadur EK Krishnan, was appointed the Deputy Collector. He was progressive and supported her education. It was not as if she chose to study or tread the unusual path from the beginning, but from childhood, she had a natural inclination towards flora and fauna. They had a small garden at their home where her father would maintain and care for all types of plants. That is how Ammal saw plants that could mean so much more than just living things rooted in soil. It was her first introduction to botany, and it sparked a love in her.

Janaki had 18 siblings and a different bond with her extended family. As her father married two ladies, they became a big but closely knit family. Janaki was the tenth child of her father's second wife. Her mother, Devi Amma, was a very kind-hearted and sweet lady. Together, they were all a flourishing and happy family that lived a comfortable life. Her brothers were known for their keen interest in cricket and were the finest 11 in a league.

Dewan Bahadur also maintained a good library at home and encouraged all his children to read and learn. His interest in ornithology, botany, and natural sciences was passed on to his children. Even though the family belonged to the Thiya community of North Malabar and came from one of the backward classes of that time, the parents, both Devi Amma and Dewan, never let any of this get in the way of their children's learning and growth. Dewan even published two books on botanical topics and was well-known for his knowledge of the field. His books on birds of the North Malabar region were quite popular.

Janaki went to the Sacred Heart Convent school in Thalassery. Being a small town with a society that generally did not support and promote schooling for girls, it was not very common for girls to excel in studies. She continued to build her interest in science and chose to pursue botany for higher studies. As she was growing up, she saw many of her sisters get married over the years. However, Janaki was able to convince her parents to let her pursue a course in botany, for which she needed to move to Madras.

She excelled in her studies and went on to earn her bachelor's degree in botany from Queen Mary's College in Madras. She also wanted to obtain an honours degree in botany from the Presidency College. At that time, higher education was not common for females in India, and this was not a regular course that women pursued. In many ways, she was already showing signs of breaking the glass ceiling in her life. After completing her graduation, Janaki decided to take up teaching at the Christ Women's College in Madras. She knew that teaching would keep her close to her interest in learning and continuing her work in the field. Though research and development in India were far behind, she understood very early that it would be best to go abroad to learn. She had the hunger to deepen her understanding and conduct groundbreaking research in the field and thus was always on the lookout for opportunities.

One big opportunity came her way, which was to study at the well-known University of Michigan. However, she needed financial support to pursue the course abroad. She applied for the Barbour Scholarship that was established by a philanthropist called Levi Barbour. This scholarship was meant for Asian women to support their studies in the USA. Unfortunately, after arriving in the US, she was detained at Ellis Island like many other immigrants. In those days, it was an unfair practice for people from colonized countries to travel freely, and that too for higher education. During the questions about immigration, it was mistakenly thought that she was an Indian Princess travelling for work. She was indeed an elegant-looking, tall woman with long dark hair. Her traditional Indian silk saree made her look graceful.

The officers set up a discussion with Janaki to assess her origins and rationale for the travel. One of the officers in the committee even inquired quite directly, "Madam, would you please indicate if you are an Indian Princess?" At first, Janaki was a little taken aback at this question. She knew that if she was not permitted, she would not be able to pursue her dream of studying further. At the cost of not losing what lay ahead of her, she decided not to deny this assumption that the immigration officers had about her. Hence, she was permitted to stay in America.

Finally, through all this, she made her way to the University of Michigan, where she was very focused on her work in Plant Cytology. This was mainly a study of the genetic composition and patterns of gene expression in plants. Over the years, she specialized in breeding interspecific hybrids (produced from plants of a different species) and intergeneric hybrids (plants of different genera within the same family). She thoroughly enjoyed her time in Michigan. She was in touch with her sister Parvathi and often wrote letters about the amazing experiences she was having.

Janaki wrote to her about the scenic beauty in Michigan. She was on a visit to the Michigan Peninsula and had never witnessed such a beautiful sight in her life. She wrote to her sister expressing her delight about the view and just how organized everything was, even though they were so disconnected from civilization. Something that had amazed Janaki was the commonalities between the experiences and perspectives of the Asians. She had always longed to be back in India, but she believed in cross-cultural exchanges. She had always thought to herself, "I am interested in India, but the whole of Asia has many common threads. I wish someday we could do some exchanges with other countries." Janaki knew that this would mean a lot of resources and investments, but she knew that it would bring so much back to the people.

In 1925, Ammal earned a Master of Science. Through her work at the University of Michigan, she obtained a PhD in 1931 as the Oriental Barbour Fellow. Her thesis was titled 'Chromosome Studies in Nicandra Physalodes'. The university also awarded her an honorary LLD in 1956. This was one of the most enriching experiences of her life as she gathered a lot of detailed insights about the field. After studying abroad for a number of years, she decided to return to Indian soil and joined as a Professor of Botany at the Maharaja's College of Science in Trivandrum. She taught at the university for two years (1932-34) as an Assistant Professor.

Eventually, Janaki decided to join the Sugarcane Breeding Station at Coimbatore. In the early 1920s, India imported the sweetest sugarcane. In those days, Papua New Guinea was one of the leading producers in the world. Under the leadership of CA Barber, the Sugarcane Breeding

Station was established. The purpose was to improve the quality of the sugarcane plants in India. Janaki dived deep into this work through her research. She spent numerous hours in the lab cross-breeding sugarcane varieties and identified a high-yielding variety that could be cultivated in India. She also identified S spontanuem as the native variety of sugarcane that had originated in India and analyzed plant varieties that were best suited for cross-breeding. Through several trials and tests, Janaki found that cross-breeding of sugarcane and maize could lead to a variety that worked in the Indian context.

Even though Janaki had worked hard for this development, the hardest part was that she did not receive any credit for it. It was indeed a male-driven world, and little was thought of the women. Her male seniors and colleagues were jealous of her contribution in such a short span of time. To top it all, Janaki knew that she came from a backward caste and could use that to raise her name, but she did not want to get lost in accolades and awards. She never let any such petty discouragements stop her from moving forward in life. She knew that her research skills and knowledge needed to continue growing. Janaki had a deep hunger to refine her learning further, and she would constantly read about the recent research in the sector. Through her research, she came across Cyril Dean Darlington. He was a well-known British Biologist who had published widely on evolution, which eventually went on to add to the role of Genetics in human history.

In 1939, Janaki got an opportunity to attend the seventh International Congress of Genetics in Edinburgh. However, things took a different turn because of World War II. Janaki was not sure about the selection of a research course for her future direction, but she was made to stay back in London for six more years. That is when Janaki decided to join the John Innes Institute in Merton, London, where she worked with CD Darlington. He was a Geneticist who was well known for his research in understanding the influence that chromosomes had in plant breeding.

During that time, Janaki got very interested in chromosome studies on a wide variety of garden plants. Through her work, she was able to deepen her understanding of the evolution of species and varieties. Janaki studied in detail the chromosome numbers and ploidy to understand the combination and effect of each. This also laid the foundation to understand how chromosomes worked within the human race. As her research progressed, CD Darlington guided her in publishing the mapping. Together, they published a very famous Chromosome Atlas of Cultivated Plants.

Janaki had identified the gap in the literature and suggested developing the same, as most of the atlases focused only on the botanical classifications. This atlas was uniquely structured as it recorded the chromosomes for about one lakh plants and provided knowledge on the breeding and evolutionary patterns of the botanical groups. Janaki deeply appreciated the partnership with CD Darlington, and together, they collaborated on long-term research work.

As time passed, Janaki felt more equipped for experimentation in the field of Chromosomal Structures and Breeding. In 1946, Janaki's career took a positive turn as she was offered a full-time role at the Royal Horticulture Society in Wisley. It was not a difficult choice for her as she was in love with botanical plants, and working as a Cytologist, she could use her past research experience for more development in the field. In the society, Janaki was the first woman employee who was kept on a salary. At the Royal Horticulture Society, she started studying the botanical use of Colchicine and how it could shape plant breeding.

The main purpose of Colchicine was to double the plant's chromosome number. This would yield larger and faster-growing plants. She started working on Magnolias to learn more about their hybridization and how the plant growth could be expedited. Janaki's research inspired her to work on Magnolias' cytology, and she started conducting experiments on their hybridization. Janaki ended up creating some unique varieties of Magnolia. One of those varieties was named—Magnolia kobus Janaki Ammal. It was a shrub with flowers of bright white petals and purple stamens. During her stint, Janaki ended up planting flowers in the garden of the Royal Horticulture Society. Little did she know that these plants would stay on for many years even after the experiments were over.

Eventually, Janaki wanted to come back to India and do something in the field of botany. In early 1950, Janaki returned to India on the special request from India's first Prime Minister, Jawaharlal Nehru. Though Janaki had been away from India for a long time, she had been closely following all the developments in the country. Prime Minister Nehru was very keen for Janaki to come back to India. Janaki heard about this personal request and thought that it was 'Indeed a time to serve the nation and go back to her roots.' India had seen a series of famines since 1943. Millions had lost their lives, and it was time to bring food security to the country. Janaki was appointed as the supervisor in charge of directing the Central Botanical Laboratory in Lucknow. She knew that the appointment would be a big responsibility, but it was her opportunity to give back to society. Nehru indicated to her advisers, "We need people like her to come back to serve their country." Janaki had felt the calling and happily took up the role. During this appointment, she was tasked with reorganizing the Botanical Survey of India (BSI), which was originally established in 1890.

Janaki knew this would not be easy, and so she started full throttle in putting together a framework for reorganizing the survey plan and structure. Through her work and future planning, she realized that some of the initiatives planned by the government were not enough to boost food production in India. She knew that a lot needed to be done to meet the consumption demands in the country. However, many of these were at the cost of conservation of the Indian ecosystem. After going through acute food shortages and famines in the 1940s, the Government of India reclaimed 25 million acres of land for the cultivation of the Grow More Food Campaign.

The purpose of this policy initiative was to increase the production of grains and other cereals in India. However, through her assessment, Janaki was abysmally disappointed as deforestation had been quite rampant and uncontrolled in the country. The peak of her disappointment came when, during an expedition to Meghalaya, Janaki had to travel 37 miles from Shillong to search for the only Magnolia Griffith tree in the North-eastern part of India. On reaching the spot, she learned that the tree had been burnt down. She was so upset about the lack of sensitivity towards the fauna in the country that she wrote to CD Darlington about the same and expressed her helplessness in the situation.

She continued her advocacy for preserving the botanical species in India. In her own capacity, Janaki decided that it would be crucial to preserve the indigenous plants that were under threat of extinction. Through her work on the BSI, she wanted to house the specimens that had been collected from across the continent in a Herbarium. She understood the value of the Botanical Survey for India and by India, as it would take an indigenous person to understand the value of plants in the country. Unfortunately, she was very disappointed to see that a European Hermenegild Santapau, had been appointed director for BSI. Janaki was very sad with the appointment because she had been denied the authority, even though she truly deserved the position.

Over time, Janaki had developed a close association with CD Darlington and would often reach out to him for professional consultations and share personal news. She needed to share her frustration with the development and so wrote to CD Darlington to share her thoughts. She wrote to him saying, "I bring you news of a major defeat for botanical science in India. The Govt. of India has appointed as the Chief Botanist of India—a man with Kew tradition and I, the director of the Central Botanical Laboratory, must now take orders from him... Kew has won … and we have lost." Despite India's independence from British rule, Britain's colonization of the country manifested in science. This was an ideological loss for Janaki, and she felt like her native skills had not been valued.

Janaki was of the view that India needed a well-organized and systematic study of the flora, which could not be done by a foreigner. Not because she doubted their ability, but would anyone with a different origin understand things the way Indian botanists would? Maybe not. And this is what pinched her immensely. She did not want to settle for this compromise, and after much deliberation, she decided to issue a memorandum on the survey and planning for the same. She expressed her dissatisfaction by saying, "The plants collected in India during the last 30 years have been chiefly by foreign botanists and often sponsored by institutions outside India. They are now found in various gardens and herbaria in Europe so that modern research on the flora of India can be conducted more intensely outside than within this country." Janaki dreaded that all indigenous knowledge would be lost like this. This was also an experience for Janaki through which she realized that she was one of the few female botanists in the world. She was also one of the few who valued the native plants and the knowledge behind them. She often wondered how to retain all this in the best interest of the country.

In 1955, Janaki went to attend the International Symposium in Chicago. Janaki could see the irony of the situation as she was the only woman to attend the symposium, which was titled 'Man's Role in Changing the Face of Earth.' At the symposium, Janaki addressed the group about India's subsistence economy, during which she highlighted the Indian setup and its history, geography, and culture. She emphasized how all these factors played an important role in the agricultural and physiological development of the region.

Janaki wanted to do so much for the BSI. Her dreams and aspirations were unmatched and could help conduct thorough mapping and conservation as per the physiological needs of the country. Unfortunately, all her requests and attempts to reorganize the survey were turned down several times. Slowly, Janaki started feeling that she was and would never be fully accepted at the institute. All this was because she was a female botanist. She was also deeply hurt by the insensitivity and disrespect for her work. With what she had started and returned to India to serve her nation had all been in vain. She could see that even her male colleagues and juniors refused to take her command. This made her realize that all her efforts to improve the Botanical Survey were at a standstill.

Simultaneously, she wanted to pursue her vision for conserving the indigenous plants. She started going on several expeditions and journeys to learn about plants in the region and what could be done to save them and their future. Janaki was always happy and delighted whenever she was in the company of plants, and so after being disappointed by the lack of developments at BSI, she moved on to working more closely on identifying the flora and fauna of the country that needed attention.

Janaki came across an exciting opportunity to travel through the remotest forests of Nepal. She was thrilled at this opportunity, as botanically Nepal was a unique part of Asia. Through the expedition, she got an opportunity to look at the rarest of plants and study them closely. Eventually, she took on a short research role at the Bhabha Atomic Research Centre at Trombay, before becoming an Emeritus Scientist at the Centre for Advanced Study in Botany at the University of Madras. During her last years, she reared a small garden in her house and kept a large family of cats and kittens.

In 1977, when she was 80, the Indian government awarded her a Padma Shri, one of the country's highest civilian honours. The University of Michigan conferred an honorary LLD on Janaki in 1956 in recognition of her contributions to botany and Cytogenetics. The award said – 'Blessed with the ability to make painstaking and accurate observations, she and her patient endeavours stand as a model for serious and dedicated scientific workers.'

In 2000, the Ministry of Environment and Forestry created the National Award of Taxonomy in her name. Janaki left her presence in the smell of Magnolia and her individuality in the sugar of Indian sugarcane, reminding us that the result of believing in oneself is often sweet. In 2018, to celebrate her remarkable career and contribution to plant science, two rose breeders, Girija and Viru Viraraghavan, bred a new rose variety, which they named EK Janaki Ammal.

Overall, Janaki faced several challenges and pushbacks in life, but from a young age, she was very courageous to make choices that were not common for any female of her age or caste. She was never let down by the male-dominated setup and was always open to adapting where and when required. All that ever mattered to her in life was her passion for plants. That is what guided her as she defined her goals and purpose in life.

3.
Kamala Sohonie

Kamala Sohonie was an Indian Biochemist who became the first Indian woman to receive a PhD in a scientific discipline.

She was an Indian biochemist who broke through barriers far stronger than academic competition. She became the first Indian woman to receive a PhD in a scientific discipline, but her journey to that milestone was neither easy nor obvious. She was born on 18 June 1911, in Indore, into a family where science was not merely a profession but almost a shared language spoken at home. Her father, Narayanrao Bhagwat, was a distinguished chemist; her uncle, Madhavrao Bhagwat, too, belonged to the rare circle of those who pursued scientific education in the early 20th century. Both had graduated from the Tata Institute of Science in Bangalore—later the Indian Institute of Science—and their stories, reflections, and respect for scientific enquiry formed a natural part of Kamala's childhood.

In those formative years, Kamala often watched her father and uncle talk passionately about their work, filled with excitement over discoveries and challenges. She noticed how confidently they spoke of scientific concepts that sounded difficult to others, yet came so naturally to them. These everyday moments inspired her deeply. From an early age, she dreamt of belonging to that same world—a world where curiosity was respected and questions were celebrated. Her school years reflected this drive; she consistently topped her class and showed signs of a sharp, analytical mind. Nobody in her family was surprised when she expressed a desire to pursue science after school. She was disciplined, hardworking, and had a natural affinity toward the subject.

Encouraged by her family, Kamala enrolled in the BSc program at Bombay Presidency College, choosing Physics and Chemistry as her dual majors. At a time when women rarely travelled far from home to study, Kamala's decision to pursue higher education outside her hometown reflects the progressive attitudes her family held, especially regarding women's education. Bombay, with its intellectual vibrancy, exposed her to new ways of thinking. In the classroom, she was earnest and meticulous; outside the classroom, she found herself drawn even more deeply to the world of biochemistry. Her interactions with professors, her readings, and her long hours in the laboratory all strengthened her belief that she wanted to pursue research.

As she approached graduation, the question of further study naturally arose. Given that both her father and uncle were alumni of the Indian Institute of Science, the family encouraged her to consider applying there. The institute had a formidable reputation—rigorous, selective, and deeply respected. But there was a problem that was well-known to anyone familiar with IISc: the institute did not admit women. The idea of a woman joining as a research student was almost inconceivable at the time. Higher education itself was rare for women in India in the early 1930s; research was practically unheard of. Yet Kamala, who had graduated with first-class marks and topped her university, felt confident that her merit would speak louder than any preconceived notions.

Her application to IISc, however, became the beginning of a painful lesson in how deeply society's patriarchal norms could overshadow even the brightest academic achievements. At the heart of the decision was Sir C.V. Raman, India's first Nobel Laureate in science, and one of the greatest physicists the world has produced. His contributions to science were monumental, yet like many men of his era, he carried unexamined social beliefs shaped by the culture he grew up in. The early 20th century was a time when Indian society, even in its most educated circles, rarely imagined women occupying advanced scientific or technical roles. Women's education was often tolerated but not always taken seriously; women pursuing careers in research were viewed as exceptions, not the norm.

Raman's rejection of Kamala's application was blunt and deeply disheartening. There was no academic explanation or assessment of her merit; It was a categorical dismissal. Accounts suggest that his response was simply, "I am not going to take any girls in my institute." His tone and stance were reflective of broader societal attitudes rather than individual animosity. The world at that time had conditioned even brilliant minds to believe that women did not belong in rigorous scientific spaces. This conditioning was so pervasive that even those who championed rationality and scientific thinking sometimes failed to step back and examine their own biases.

For Kamala, the rejection was a bewildering confrontation she had not expected to face. For a young woman who had grown up surrounded by scientific discussion, encouraged by her family, and rewarded academically at every stage, the idea that her gender could shut the doors of opportunity was both unexpected and painful. She must have wondered, as many women did in that era, how much harder she would have to fight for opportunities that her male counterparts received automatically. And if she, with her privilege of an educated family, faced this obstacle, what must have been the plight of women with fewer resources, fewer opportunities, and fewer voices to speak on their behalf?

Her father and uncle, shocked by the rejection, decided to appeal directly to the institute. As alumni, they believed that their presence might at least prompt a fair hearing. But even they soon discovered that the obstacle was not bureaucratic, it was ideological. Raman was unwavering in his stance. He was unwilling to consider exceptions, unwilling to listen to arguments about Kamala's merit, and unwilling to imagine that a woman could thrive in an environment he believed was suited only for men. It was a painful moment for the family, and especially for Kamala, who had to come to terms with the fact that brilliance alone was not enough to transcend societal expectations.

But Kamala was not someone who retreated in the face of adversity. Rather than giving up, she decided to confront Raman herself, not out of rebellion, but out of a desire for fairness and reason. She went to his office repeatedly, hoping that personal interaction might sway his judgment. In these moments, Kamala displayed remarkable courage and poise. Many women at the time would not have dared to question a man of Raman's stature. But Kamala's questions were honest, persistent, and rooted in her belief that science could only benefit from more curious minds, regardless of gender.

Day after day, she returned. What she engaged in was a personal satyagraha... a peaceful, everyday assertion of her right to be heard. Raman, at first unmoved, gradually began to see her persistence as a reflection of genuine commitment. He finally relented, but his decision came with conditions that revealed both the limitations of the time and the conflicted nature of his own beliefs. Kamala was granted admission, but only on probation. She would not be treated as a regular student. Her performance would be scrutinized more closely than that of any other student, and any 'disturbance' caused by her presence could lead to immediate expulsion.

These conditions were undoubtedly discriminatory. Yet they also reveal Raman's struggle to reconcile the norms he had inherited with the evidence of Kamala's merit and determination. Kamala accepted the conditions not out of helplessness, but out of her willingness to work harder, prove herself, and create space for others who would come after her.

Once admitted, Kamala threw herself wholeheartedly into her research. Working with the esteemed Professor M. Sreenivasaya, she found a mentor who recognised her sincerity and intellectual capability. Under his guidance, she worked on characterizing proteins from food sources such as milk, legumes, and pulses. Her research on pulse proteins and Non-Protein-Nitrogen captured early insights into nutritional science, especially relevant for children and people with limited access to diverse foods. Within a few years, she became the only scientist studying pulse protein at such depth. Her work was not only academically significant but also socially relevant in a country where malnutrition was widespread.

Her success and dedication slowly challenged the very assumptions that had originally kept her out of the institute. Her work made it impossible for IISc to ignore the contributions women could make. Within a year of her joining, the institute opened its doors to female students: a historic shift that was both symbolic and practical. Kamala had not only proven herself; she had expanded the horizon of possibilities for women scientists across India. Her perseverance had quietly shifted an institution.

After completing her Master's degree, Kamala joined the Haffkine Institute in Bombay, where she continued her work on enzymes. Her research experience caught the attention of Cambridge University, where she applied for a scholarship. She was accepted, and this marked another turning point in her life. At Cambridge, she worked with Dr Derek Richter and later with Dr Robin Hill, on projects involving amine oxidases and plant tissue respiration. Her research led to fascinating discoveries, including her detailed characterization of cytochrome C in plant tissues. Her findings were published in Nature in

1939, a rare honour for any researcher, especially a woman from India at that time.

Her PhD thesis, completed in just sixteen months, was praised for its precision and clarity. At a time when dissertations often ran into hundreds of pages, Kamala's elegantly concise 40-page thesis stood out. She became the first Indian woman to receive a PhD in science; a milestone not just for her, but for the generations of women who would follow.

Although she received several lucrative offers from American pharmaceutical companies after completing her PhD, Kamala made the extraordinary decision to return to India. At a time when India was simmering with the energies of the freedom movement, she felt a sense of responsibility toward her country. Her admiration for Gandhian principles and her desire to serve the nation guided her choice. She believed that her scientific training should contribute to India and its people.

Upon returning in 1939, she took up a professorship at Lady Hardinge Medical College in Delhi, but the lack of infrastructure and support limited the scope of her work. Soon after, she moved to the Nutrition Research Laboratory in Coonoor, where she became deeply involved in studies related to vitamins, amino acids, and nutritional deficiencies. Her work contributed to the scientific understanding of malnutrition in India, especially among vulnerable groups.

During this time, she also began receiving marriage proposals, and it was then that she met Madhav Sohonie, a scholar of actuarial science. The two developed respect and affection for each other over their intellectual conversations. After seeking her family's approval, they married, and Kamala moved to Bombay in 1947. She embraced motherhood with as much dedication as she had shown in the laboratory. Her sons, Anil and Jayant, fondly remember her as someone who brought warmth, discipline, and tenderness to their home, despite her demanding academic life.

In the years that followed, Kamala joined the Royal Institute of Science in Bombay as a Professor of Biochemistry. Here, she focused on foods commonly consumed by India's economically weaker sections. She and her students analysed legumes, fish, vegetables, and other staple foods to understand their nutritional value. This research eventually led her to one of her most impactful projects—studying *neera,* the nutritious sap extracted from palm trees. The project was initiated at the suggestion of Dr Rajendra Prasad, who saw potential in turning this widely available natural resource into an accessible nutritional supplement for the poor.

Kamala approached the project with rigour. She discovered that neera was rich in vitamin C, B vitamins, and crucial sulfhydryl compounds that protected nutrients even when the drink was stored. She and her students travelled across various states to study regional varieties and conducted field tests on pregnant women and malnourished tribal children. Her findings revealed remarkable improvements in health among those who consumed neera regularly. This research not only offered a low-cost solution for improving nutrition among vulnerable communities but also laid the foundation for recognising neera as a scientifically validated health drink. For her contribution, Kamala received the Rashtrapati Award.

Despite her contributions, Kamala continued to face gender bias within academic institutions. She was denied the position of Director at the Institute where she worked, despite being the most qualified candidate. This discrimination, however, did not diminish her dedication to research. She continued guiding students, writing papers, and advocating for nutritional interventions for the poor. Kamala was also an active member of the Consumer Guidance Society of India, where she worked passionately on issues related to food quality and consumer safety. She wrote extensively for the organisation's magazine and worked tirelessly to raise awareness about nutrition and food adulteration.

In her final years, recognition for her life's work finally began to gather momentum. Dr Satyavathi, the first woman Director-General of ICMR, having learned of Kamala's struggles and achievements, organised a ceremony to honour her. Kamala attended the event at the age of 84, deeply moved by the recognition she had long deserved. Tragically, she collapsed during the event and passed away shortly after.

Her life story is not just one of scientific achievement, but of resilience against deeply entrenched societal biases. Reflecting on her early years at IISc, she once said, "Though Raman was a great scientist, he was very narrow-minded. I can never forget the way he treated me just because I was a woman." Yet even in this statement, there was no bitterness—only a clear-eyed recognition of the truth. Her experience with Raman was not a clash between individuals, but a reflection of the time they lived in. Raman was a genius in physics, but he was shaped by a society that limited women. Kamala, on the other hand, represented a new wave of women who would challenge and transform those limitations.

Her journey stands as a powerful reminder that progress often happens because someone refuses to accept the boundaries placed before them. Kamala's courage opened the doors of Indian science to countless women after her. Her legacy endures not only in academic literature but in the confidence of every young woman who steps into a laboratory today, knowing she belongs there because women like Kamala did not step back.

4.
Asima Chatterjee

Asima Chatterjee was an Indian Organic Chemist who was noted for her work in the fields of Organic Chemistry and Phytomedicine.

Asima, a pioneering figure in the realm of Organic Chemistry and Phytomedicine, emerged from humble beginnings in colonial India to become a trailblazer in the scientific community. Despite facing numerous challenges as a woman in a male-dominated field, Chatterjee's unwavering determination, intellect, and passion for scientific inquiry propelled her to overcome obstacles and leave an indelible mark in the fields of Organic Chemistry and Phytomedicine.

Asima was born in Kolkata, India, on 23 September 1917. She defied societal norms and gender barriers to pursue her passion for chemistry, thus ultimately revolutionizing the fields of Organic Chemistry and Phytomedicine through her groundbreaking research and discoveries.

She had one sister, and both of them were encouraged to get an education, which was a rarity at that time. Asima Chatterjee's childhood was shaped by a unique blend of intellectual stimulations and familial support, thereby laying the groundwork for her remarkable journey in the field of science. Growing up in Kolkata, then Calcutta, during the early 20th century, Asima was surrounded by a rich cultural milieu and a society that was undergoing profound changes. Despite the prevailing societal norms that relegated women to traditional roles, Asima's upbringing was marked by a spirit of progressive thinking, which was fostered by her parents.

As the daughter of Dr Indra Narayan Mukherjee, a respected lecturer of chemistry at Calcutta University, and Kamala Devi, who hailed from a family of scholars, Asima was immersed in an environment that valued education and intellectual pursuits. Her parents recognized her innate curiosity and encouraged her to explore the world around her with a thirst for knowledge that knew no bounds. At home, Asima's father took an active role in her education by instilling in her a love for learning and a sense of intellectual inquisitiveness from a young age. He provided her with books on a wide range of subjects, thus fostering her natural inclination towards academic pursuits and nurturing her burgeoning intellect. Her parents recognized her intellectual potential and encouraged her to pursue her studies. Her family's opinion was that 'If you educate a woman, you educate a nation.'

Growing up in colonial India, Asima Chatterjee faced numerous challenges, which included limited educational opportunities for women. Asima's formal education commenced at the renowned Bethune College in Kolkata, where she enrolled for her undergraduate studies in chemistry. Despite facing financial constraints, she excelled in her studies, demonstrating exceptional academic prowess and a passion for the subject. Her dedication and diligence earned her the admiration of her professors and peers alike, setting her apart as a promising young scholar.

As she had demonstrated a keen interest in learning, even though there were financial constraints, she continued her education, earning a master's degree in chemistry from the University of Calcutta. These formative years laid the groundwork for Chatterjee's future achievements in the field of organic chemistry. This period marked a crucial juncture in her life, as she delved deeper into the intricacies of organic chemistry and began to explore her research interests in natural products and medicinal plants.

As Asima Chatterjee progressed in her academic journey, her passion for chemistry and dedication to learning continued to shine brightly. After completing her undergraduate studies, she embarked on a pioneering endeavour that further cemented her place in history. In 1940, Asima joined Lady Brabourne College (one of the prestigious colleges in Kolkata) as the Founder-Head of the Department of Chemistry. In 1944, she was appointed Honorary Lecturer in the Department of Chemistry, University of Calcutta.

Asima Chatterjee achieved a significant milestone by becoming the first woman to receive a Doctorate of Science (DSc) in 1944 from an Indian university. This monumental achievement took place at the prestigious University of Calcutta, marking a historic moment not only for Chatterjee but also for women in academia across India.

During her DSc, she worked with Professor Prafulla Chandra Ray, and her doctoral thesis included rigorous research and scholarly inquiry. In her thesis, she explored the chemical composition of Aristolochia indica, a medicinal plant commonly used in traditional Indian medicine. The nature of Chatterjee's doctoral research extended beyond its scientific significance. By earning her DSc, she shattered gender barriers and defied societal expectations, thereby proving that women were just as capable as men in the pursuit of advanced academic degrees. She went on to be acknowledged as the Doyenne of Chemistry.

She specialized in synthetic organic chemistry and plant products as part of her doctoral research. Her research was directed by Professor Prafulla Kumar Bose, one of the pioneers in Natural Product Chemistry in India. She was privileged to be in close contact with some experts in Indian sciences like Acharya Prafulla Chandra Ray, Professor Prafulla Chandra Mitra, and Professor Jitendra Nath Mukherjee, who influenced her career and thinking as a Natural Product Scientist. Her interest in organic chemistry began at this stage, as she was herself unaware of the things that she would go on to discover.

Chatterjee's achievement served as a beacon of inspiration for aspiring female scientists, demonstrating that gender should never be a barrier to academic success. Her accomplishments paved the way for future generations of women in academia, empowering them to pursue their academic and scientific aspirations with confidence and determination. Furthermore, Chatterjee's DSc not only symbolized her individual triumph but also represented a significant step forward for Indian science. Her pioneering research laid the foundation for future advancements in Organic Chemistry and Phytomedicine, thus contributing to the advancement of scientific knowledge and the betterment of society.

Overall, Asima Chatterjee's attainment of a Doctorate of Science at the University of Calcutta in 1944 stands as a testament to her intellectual brilliance, unwavering perseverance, and determination. Her pioneering achievements continue to inspire generations of scientists, particularly women, to push the boundaries of knowledge and strive for excellence in their respective fields.

This was also a time of some personal development for Asima as she got married. Asima Chatterjee's marriage to Professor Baradananda Chatterjee marked a significant milestone in her personal life, adding a new dimension to her already illustrious career as a scientist. The union between Asima, a trailblazing chemist, and Baradananda, an esteemed academic, was characterized by mutual respect, intellectual companionship, and shared values.

Baradananda Chatterjee, a prominent figure in the academic community, was a distinguished scholar known for his expertise in his field. His support for Asima's academic pursuits and his encouragement of her scientific endeavours played a crucial role in her professional success. Their marriage was a partnership that was built on mutual admiration, shared aspirations, and a deep commitment to each other's personal and professional growth.

Despite the demands of their respective careers, Asima and Baradananda found a harmonious balance between work and family life. As dedicated academics, they understood the importance of supporting each other's ambitions and aspirations, while also prioritizing their roles as parents and partners. A few years after their marriage, Asima gave birth to a beautiful daughter whom they named Julie.

Julie Chatterjee grew up in a household which was steeped in intellectual curiosity and academic excellence. From an early age, she was exposed to the world of science and scholarship, while being surrounded by her parents' passion for knowledge and discovery. Asima and Baradananda instilled a deep appreciation for education and the pursuit of excellence in Julie, thus nurturing her natural curiosity and encouraging her to explore her interests. Growing up under the guidance of two accomplished academics, Julie was inspired by her parents' dedication to their work and their unwavering commitment to the advancement of knowledge. Their home was a nurturing environment where Julie's intellectual inquisitiveness was stimulated, and she was encouraged to pursue her own academic and personal aspirations.

After achieving significant milestones in her personal life in India, Asima Chatterjee sought to expand her horizons further and deepen her knowledge by embarking on an academic journey abroad. Dr (Mrs) Chatterjee left for the USA in 1947 on a study leave from Lady Brabourne College. One of the pivotal moments in her career was when she had the opportunity to work with Professor László Zechmeister, a renowned chemist, at both the University of Wisconsin and the California Institute of Technology (Caltech).

Chatterjee's collaboration with Zechmeister provided her with invaluable insights and exposure to cutting-edge research in the field of organic chemistry, particularly in the chemistry of biologically active alkaloids. These are naturally occurring organic compounds which are found in plants that often possess pharmacological properties.

During her time at the University of Wisconsin and Caltech, Chatterjee immersed herself in the study of alkaloids by focusing on their isolation, characterization, and synthesis. Alkaloids are naturally occurring organic compounds that possess pharmacological effects on the human body. Recognizing the therapeutic potential of alkaloids, Chatterjee directed her research efforts toward isolating, identifying, and synthesizing these biologically active compounds from various plant sources. Under Zechmeister's mentorship, she honed her skills in organic synthesis and spectroscopic techniques, thereby gaining hands-on experience in the laboratory and collaborating with fellow researchers.

Chatterjee's research during this period led to several noteworthy discoveries in the chemistry of alkaloids, which included the synthesis of novel compounds and the elucidation of their chemical structures. Her work contributed to the growing body of knowledge surrounding alkaloids and their potential applications in medicine and pharmacology. One of Chatterjee's notable contributions during her post-doctoral research was her investigation into the alkaloids which are present in the Vinca rosea plant, commonly known as the Madagascar periwinkle. This plant has long been used in traditional medicine for its purported medicinal properties, particularly in the treatment of diabetes and cancer. Through meticulous experimentation and analysis, Chatterjee successfully isolated and identified several alkaloids from Vinca rosea, which included vinblastine and vincristine. These alkaloids were found to exhibit potent anti-cancer properties, thus paving the way for the development of life-saving chemotherapy drugs that are used in the treatment of various forms of cancer, including leukaemia and lymphoma.

Chatterjee's research on biologically active alkaloids extended beyond Vinca rosea to encompass other medicinal plants which are indigenous to India. Her work contributed to the elucidation of the chemical structures of numerous alkaloids and their pharmacological effects, thereby further expanding our understanding of the natural products in medicine.

In addition to her laboratory investigations, Chatterjee also collaborated with pharmacologists and medical researchers to evaluate the efficacy and safety of the alkaloid-based drugs in clinical settings. Her interdisciplinary approach to research bridged the gap between chemistry and medicine, thus leading to the development of novel treatments for a wide range of diseases.

The impact of Asima Chatterjee's post-doctoral research on biologically active alkaloids reverberated throughout the scientific community, thus revolutionizing the field of pharmacology and transforming the landscape of modern medicine. Her groundbreaking discoveries paved the way for the development of life-saving drugs and underscored the immense potential of natural products in combating diseases.

Asima took on several challenges while pursuing her studies in the US. She showed considerable courage in taking her eleven-month-old daughter with her, along with a governess. Apart from studying, this was also the place where Asima got acquainted with thoughtful leaders from India. She came into close contact with the Late Swami Nikhilanandaji Maharaj and the late Swami Prabhabanandaji Maharaj of the Ramakrishna-Vivekananda Centres in the USA. Thus began her life-long association with them and subsequently with the Ramakrishna Math and Mission, in Belur, West Bengal. Late Swami Abhayanandaji Maharaj (the seniormost vice-president of the Ramakrishna Order; popularly known as Bharat Maharaj) and Late Swami Rangathanandaji

Maharaj (former president of the Ramakrishna Order) Ramakrishna Math and Mission, Belur, played a dominant role in her life by providing inspiration and courage.

After completing her doctoral studies, Asima Chatterjee's academic journey led her to a prominent position at the University College of Science, University of Calcutta. In recognition of her scholarly achievements and groundbreaking research, she was appointed a Reader in Pure Chemistry, thereby marking a significant milestone in her career. As a Reader in Pure Chemistry, Chatterjee assumed a pivotal role in the academic community, where she dedicated herself to both teaching and research. Her appointment underscored her expertise in the field of organic chemistry and her contributions to the advancement of scientific knowledge.

In her capacity as a Reader, Chatterjee played a vital role in shaping the next generation of chemists and researchers. She shared her wealth of knowledge and expertise with students by imparting valuable insights into the principles and practices of organic chemistry. Her passion for teaching and mentorship inspired countless students to pursue careers in science and follow in her footsteps. She faced many challenges during her tenure at the University College of Science. As a woman in a predominantly male-dominated field, Chatterjee faced significant gender discrimination throughout her career. Despite her remarkable academic achievements and contributions to the field of chemistry, she encountered scepticism and prejudice from her male colleagues and superiors. This gender bias manifested in various forms, which included unequal opportunities for advancement, limited access to resources and funding, and exclusion from the decision-making processes within the academic institution.

At the peak of her career, she also became the Head of the Department of Chemistry at the University of Calcutta, a post she continued till

1979. Due to her untiring efforts, understanding, effective coordination with her colleagues, and under her dynamic leadership and foresight, the department earned an international reputation as a leading Centre for Teaching and Research in Chemistry. Professor Asima Chatterjee was not satisfied with merely transmitting the facts of science to her students; thus, she instilled in them an awareness of the significance of all they were learning. She wanted them to be aware of the power that comes with the research that these students conducted. However, to convince her students about this, she also needed clear thinking and a strong art of communication, which is a very rare skill to have, especially as a woman scientist.

She was a bold and brave scientist who always fought for space for research and science in the changing landscape of India. In one of her public addresses as the General President, at the sixty-second session of the Indian Science Congress in Delhi Biographical Memoirs, she proudly placed the need for academic institutes in research by stating, "Universities constitute the backbone of Scientific and Technological Training and University Research still forms the spearhead of scientific progress and provides a reasonably good barometer to the Standard of Science and Technology in the country. Hence, universities should receive top national priority". She was well aware of several resource and infrastructural challenges that she faced at the university and did not want that to become the status quo for her students.

The University College of Science at the University of Calcutta, like many academic institutions in India during Chatterjee's time, faced challenges in terms of limited resources and infrastructure. As a result, Chatterjee had to contend with inadequate laboratory facilities, equipment, and funding for her research endeavours. She continued her research on the nature of biologically active compounds found in medicinal plants. At that time, it was very difficult for scientists to work due to fewer funds from the government, and Asima had to invest her own money to send samples for analysis outside India. She struggled to get the necessary chemicals and reagents for her research and was barely able to pay salaries to her students.

She had a grant of Rs 300 per annum and three college teachers as part-time research students. She had only one full-time scholar with a laboratory grant of Rs 1,000 per annum with a princely WB Govt stipend of Rs 150 per month. For milling plant materials, her team had to go to a faraway workshop of Jadavpur University. Even for UV measurements, her team had to go to the adjacent Bose Institute, where only Asima was allowed to handle the equipment. Her team borrowed solvents for the extraction of plant material mostly from the comparatively well-off BC Guha's laboratory, as the research grant of even the Heads of Departments was only Rs 1,200. During those hard days, she received encouragement from Professor Satyen Bose, Meghnath Saha, SK Mitra, BC Guha, Sir JC Ghosh, and other Vice-Chancellors of Calcutta University. Her husband, Professor Baradananda Chatterjee, a renowned Physical chemist himself and the Vice-Principal of the then Bengal Engineering College (now a Deemed University), Sibpur, Howrah, solidly stood by her.

As a woman in a male-dominated field, Asima Chatterjee encountered scepticism, discrimination, and institutional biases throughout her career. Despite these challenges, she remained undeterred, drawing strength from her passion for science and her unwavering commitment to excellence. Chatterjee's resilience and determination enabled her to overcome societal barriers and pave the way for future generations of women in science.

The hierarchical structure and bureaucratic nature of academic institutions presented additional challenges for Chatterjee in her role as a Reader. Institutional barriers, such as rigid academic policies, administrative red tape, and entrenched power dynamics, hindered her ability to implement innovative teaching methods, secure research grants, and advance her career within the university hierarchy.

While things were challenging professionally, she also faced a huge setback in the early years of her work at the university. She had to take a temporary break in the year 1967, because of the sudden demise of her father and her husband within a span of four months. Not being able to accept such a shock, Dr Chatterjee suffered a massive heart attack at the University of Calcutta, and the situation was so critical that she had to be hospitalized. Her father, Dr Indra Narayan Mukherjee, was the biggest pillar of support in Dr Chatterjee's life as he was a continuous source of inspiration and motivation throughout her upbringing. He was the first to notice the spark in his daughter's character and also appreciated her desire to fulfil her academic accomplishments.

As if this was not enough, while she was recovering from the loss of her father, she was suddenly hit by another major setback when she lost her husband. The sudden demise of Dr Baradananda Chatterjee, her ardent supporter, left her in a terrible shock. She faced a severe low in her life as she moved between life and death for several days. During this period of trial, she received a lot of support and prayers from her colleagues and students. It was their support and her interest in contributing meaningfully to societal development that helped her survive these challenges.

However, she continued to push through these challenges and achieved some major milestones at the university. One of Asima Chatterjee's major discoveries during her tenure at the University of Calcutta was her pioneering work on the development of anti-malarial drugs from natural sources. Chatterjee's research in this area led to the identification and synthesis of novel compounds with potent anti-malarial properties, thus making a significant contribution to the global fight against malaria, a disease that continues to take a heavy toll on human health worldwide.

Chatterjee's interest in anti-malarial research was sparked by the urgent need for effective treatments for malaria, particularly in regions where the disease was endemic and resistant strains of the malaria parasite were emerging. Drawing upon her expertise in organic chemistry and her deep understanding of medicinal plants, Chatterjee embarked on a quest to identify natural compounds with anti-malarial activity.

One of Chatterjee's most significant discoveries came in the form of a compound that was derived from the East Indian rosewood tree, scientifically known as *Holarrhena antidysenterica*. Through meticulous experimentation and chemical analysis, Chatterjee isolated and identified the active ingredient, which was responsible for the plant's anti-malarial properties. Subsequent research led to the synthesis of several analogues and derivatives of the natural compound, thus resulting in the development of new anti-malarial drugs with enhanced efficacy and reduced toxicity. These synthetic compounds showed remarkable promise in laboratory tests, while demonstrating potent anti-malarial activity against various strains of the malaria parasite.

Chatterjee's groundbreaking research on anti-malarial drugs from natural sources represented a significant breakthrough in the field of Medicinal Chemistry. Her discoveries paved the way for the development of new and improved treatments for malaria, thereby offering hope to millions of people affected by this devastating disease. Moreover, Chatterjee's work exemplified the immense potential of natural products in drug discovery and development. By harnessing the power of nature's pharmacopoeia, she demonstrated the value of traditional medicinal plants as a rich source of bioactive compounds with therapeutic potential.

Chatterjee successfully developed the anti-epileptic drug, Ayush-56, from *Marsilia minuta* and the anti-malarial drug from *Alstonia scholaris, Swertia chirata, Picrorhiza kurroa* and *Caesalpinia crista*. This life-saving invention was one of the biggest contributions that Dr Asima made towards saving mankind. The drug was eventually patented and marketed by several pharmaceutical companies to save the lives of many fellow citizens.

Her dream was to not let anyone suffer from a lack of resources and to be able to study. In 1971, she went on to establish the Regional Research Institute Ayurveda, Calcutta, which is now called the National Research Institute of Ayurvedic Drug Development (NRIADD), which includes an Ayurvedic hospital and centres for research in chemistry, botany, and pharmacology of drugs that are isolated from Indian medicinal plants.

In recognition of the work carried out in the Organic Section of the Department of Chemistry, the University Grants Commission sanctioned in 1972 the Programme of Special Assistance to selected departments for intensifying teaching and research on Natural Product Chemistry with Professor Asima Chatterjee as its Honorary Programme-Coordinator. She continued at this post till 2003.

Throughout her illustrious career, Asima Chatterjee received numerous accolades and honours for her contributions to science, which included the prestigious Shanti Swarup Bhatnagar Prize for Science and Technology. Her legacy as a pioneering female scientist continues to inspire generations of researchers, particularly women, to pursue careers in STEM fields and push the boundaries of scientific knowledge. Chatterjee's work has had a profound impact on healthcare and academia, thus shaping the development of new drugs and therapies and advancing our understanding of the medicinal properties of natural compounds.

Asima went on to receive the Padma Bhushan Award as the first female awardee in 1975. She made important contributions in the field of Medicinal Chemistry with special reference to alkaloids, coumarins, and terpenoids, analytical chemistry, and mechanistic organic chemistry. She published around 400 papers in national and international journals and more than a score of review articles in reputed serial volumes. Her publications have been extensively cited, and much of her work has been included in several textbooks. Chatterjee also edited and revised the six-volume *Bharatiya Banoushadhi* that was published by Calcutta University. She was the Chief Editor of the six-volume series, *The Treatise of Indian Medicinal Plants,* published by Council of Scientific & Industrial Research (CSIR). She was also nominated by the President of India as a member of the Rajya Sabha from February 1982 to May 1990.

Working all through her life, Asima Chatterjee brought immense passion to every role or responsibility that she took on. She continued to read about her field till her body permitted. She died on 22 November 2006, in a nursing home in Kolkata at the age of eighty-nine. She inspired and influenced many lives during and even after her life. Her philosophy and desire in life was to contribute to science as long as she could. She even expressed this by saying, "I wish to work as long as I live." In many ways, she was a woman who fought through several challenges and was still the first in achievement and did many things.

Asima Chatterjee's life and achievements serve as a testament to the transformative power of perseverance, intellect, and passion in overcoming obstacles and making a lasting impact on society. Her pioneering research in Organic Chemistry and Phytomedicine has left an indelible mark on the scientific community, revolutionizing the fields of healthcare and academia. As we reflect on Chatterjee's remarkable legacy, we continue to honour her memory by striving for excellence and fostering inclusivity and diversity in scientific inquiry. She formed deep bonds with her students and colleagues as she worked selflessly and tirelessly to take science and research to higher grounds.

Dr SC Prakashi, one of her PhD students, recalls: "Being one of her early PhD students, I have closely witnessed her initial struggles to establish herself. Those were trying days for research, particularly in the most ill-equipped university laboratories with inadequate chemicals and meagre financial assistance. Institutions such as the Department of Science and Technology or Department of Biotechnology under the Government of India were yet to come up, and the CSIR was in the formative stage." In one of her letters to Professor Chatterjee's daughter, the Late Dr Madhuri R Shah, Former Chairman of the University Grants Commission, wrote: "Her selfless devotion inspires and gives strength to people like me and renews my faith in the goodness of human nature."

Asima Chatterjee's research in Organic Chemistry and Phytomedicine revolutionized the scientific understanding of natural compounds and their therapeutic potential. Her pioneering work focused on the synthesis and characterization of chemical compounds derived from medicinal plants that are indigenous to India. Chatterjee's research encompassed a wide range of topics, which included the synthesis of anti-malarial, anti-epileptic, and anti-cancer drugs, as well as the isolation and identification of novel bioactive molecules.

5.

Rajeshwari Chatterjee

Rajeshwari Chatterjee was the first woman engineer from Karnataka and established herself as an Engineering Scientist.

India has come far in many metrics since its independence. While development is an all-round entity, many things are beginning to become a norm which were not common back in the day. One of the key areas of our backwardness was education, and more so for women who wanted to study and explore. It was never easy and became extremely difficult for women who wanted to study science. This was not only because there was a lack of societal support, but also because there was a lack of belief and faith in women and what they could defy or rather, achieve.

Rajeshwari Chatterjee was one such woman who went on to achieve many things in life and, more importantly, set an example for a number of women to follow her in the field of engineering in India. Rajeshwari was born into a progressive and supportive family. Her family was well-read and indulged in intellectual learning and sharing. Her father, BM Shivaramaiah, an advocate in Nanjangud, was the younger brother of the Kannada literary giant, Prof BM Srikantaiah. Most of Rajeshwari Chatterjee 's early life was shaped by a family environment that fostered intellectual curiosity, academic excellence, and a progressive outlook.

Rajeshwari was born on the fourth of January 1922 into a large, but open-minded family. While her family was not particularly rich, she was fortunate to grow up surrounded by individuals who valued education and encouraged participation in various activities, regardless of gender.

This was a big blessing for her and helped her in pursuing her dreams and interests in studying.

Besides having a supportive family, she also had the privilege of great female visionaries as part of her family. One big example was her grandmother, Kamalamma Dasappa, who was a trailblazer for women's education. In her time, her grandmother was one of the first women graduates in her region in the Mysore State. Kamalamma was deeply involved in promoting education for girls, especially those facing societal challenges such as widowhood or desertion. Rajeshwari called her grandmother a "social reformer for women in India". She undertook several initiatives, such as the establishment of an accelerated school syllabus, thus enabling students to complete their matriculation at a young age.

Her grandmother worked at all levels, which included policy to set up infrastructure and change norms to support accelerated schooling for girls. This was not an easy feat for anyone, especially for women at that time. Rajeshwari grew up in this household and continued to be inspired by similar thinking. It was this forward thinking and devotion to societal well-being that were ingrained in Rajeshwari at a very young age.

This initiative not only benefited Rajeshwari but also some of her cousins in the family. During their time, they were able to undergo the Special English School's curriculum run by the Mahila Seva Samaja in Basavangudi, Bangalore. This foundational learning set Rajeshwari way ahead in her career and, more importantly, in her learning appetite and hunger. Through her education, Rajeshwari picked up reading and wanted to take up history for her graduation.

Rajeshwari loved reading and learning about the developments of past events and how they informed and shaped the current status of mankind. However, she was also interested in studying science and mathematics for their logical thinking and calculative understanding.

During her early years, Rajeshwari's interest in science was nurtured by her family, particularly her grandmother, who encouraged her to pursue higher studies. In a time when few women dared to pursue careers in science, Rajeshwari's determination and ambition set her apart.

Eventually, Rajeshwari went on to pursue physics and mathematics in college. Her educational journey started with a strong foundation in mathematics and physics. She completed her BSc (Hons) and MSc in mathematics and physics from Central College, Bangalore, setting the stage for her future pursuits in the field of science and engineering. Rajeshwari Chatterjee's college life was marked by academic excellence and a passion for learning. As she pursued her higher education at the Central College Bangalore, she continued to be intrigued by the details of science and how it influenced lives on a day-to-day basis.

While Rajeshwari was in the first year, Professor CV Raman, who was the Head of the Department of Physics at IISc, was the chief guest at a function of the Mathematical Society. This was her first encounter with him. He delivered a scholarly lecture on a subject that she did not understand at all. During her time at Central College, Rajeshwari distinguished herself as a diligent and dedicated student, earning top honours and securing first position in Mysore University.

Her academic achievements during her college years reflected her innate intellectual prowess and her commitment to academic excellence. Despite societal challenges and limited opportunities for women in higher education during that time, Rajeshwari's determination and thirst for knowledge propelled her forward. Her graduation from Central College marked a significant milestone in her educational journey, thus laying the groundwork for her subsequent achievements in the field of engineering.

Rajeshwari went on to receive the Mummadi Krishnaraja Wodeyar Award, MT Narayana Iyengar Prize, and the Walters Memorial Prize for her performances in the BSc and MSc examinations at the college. Armed with a strong academic background and a passion for learning, she embarked on the path of exploration and discovery. After completing her BSc (Hons) and MSc in mathematics and physics from Central College, Bangalore, Rajeshwari started thinking about the best options to delve further into the subjects.

This was also the time when World War II was raging in Europe and North Africa, and so, it was hard to assess the turn of events. In such times, Rajeshwari thought to herself, "I wish very much to go abroad to England or the USA for higher studies in mathematics to obtain a PhD, but it is not possible during wartime." The next best thing she knew was IISc, and so she decided to join that institute for research. She knew that there was no mathematics department there, but mathematics was required to understand some problems in physics. Rajeshwari decided to meet Sir CV Raman and requested him to take her as a research student.

It was very unfortunate for her that when CV Raman found out that Rajeshwari's degree was in mathematics, he told her that he only wanted candidates who had an MSc in Physics with a high first class. This left her in shock as she knew that before going abroad, she would need to further her understanding of the subject. She had to keep learning and deepen her understanding, as she was quite firm about going abroad at the end of the war. The only other option for higher studies in India was Calcutta, but that was too far from Bangalore.

Though Rajeshwari knew that there were very good mathematicians who could guide her in her PhD degree, this was where gender-based challenges came into play. She knew that it would be very easy for a young male to make this decision, but for her, as a young female, in an era where it was not just about family support but also societal norms, it was not an easy decision. She knew that the best thing for her to build a foundation was IISc.

This is where she knew that working with the physics department would not be possible, so it would be best if she considered applying for a three-year certificate course in the Department of Electrical Technology. After she put in an application to this department, she was called for an interview by Professor SP Chakravarthy, who was the head of this department. Little did Rajeshwari know that this would be an eye-opening experience about how little support women received in the field of science in India.

When Rajeshwari went to meet Professor Chakravarthy, they had an interesting discussion about the role and challenges that would come her way. He said, "Though you are very well qualified to do this course, you would find it very difficult to go for summer practical training in far-away hot places like Calcutta and Jamshedpur because you would be the only woman among 20 young men." Rajeshwari knew that at that time, there were no industries in Bangalore, so travel would be imminent for her research work.

The Hindustan Aeronautics had just been established, but they were not taking any students for training. However, Professor Chakravarthy was supportive and willing to take Rajeshwari as a research student on a scholarship of Rs 40 per month. At that point in time, Rajeshwari contemplated the value of taking on this work for her future endeavours. She knew that this way she could learn Electronics and Electrical Communication Engineering (ECE), work on some research problems on electron tube circuits, and publish a few papers. This foundation work in the fast-growing subject of electronics would help her in obtaining a scholarship to go abroad for further studies after the end of the war. Rajeshwari accepted Professor Chakravarthy's suggestion because he was a knowledgeable man who had a master's degree from London University, UK, and who had done some research work at Calcutta University before coming to Bangalore. She knew that this opportunity would give her valuable experience for future work in this stream.

In 1943, she joined the Institute as a research scholar in Prof SP Chakravarty's lab at the Department of Electrical Technology. At this point, she had learned the theoretical details of science and mathematics, and it was important for her to learn things firsthand in electrical technology. Even though there were very few females who wanted to pursue a career in science, Rajeshwari continued to work on building her understanding to specialize in science.

During this period as a junior researcher, Rajeshwari worked on electronics, specializing in ultra-high frequency measurements. While earlier women were not encouraged to participate and be involved in IISc, the trend had slowly started changing. All this was under the leadership of CV Raman. Historically, he had objected to admitting women to the field of science at IISc. He gained a lot of negative publicity for not admitting Kamala Sohonie into IISc, even though she had done extremely well in her graduation. As time started evolving in 1940, a handful of women scientists had started making their way into the institute, but it was not all rosy for them, as they had to struggle with not only a lack of research infrastructure and resources for women, but also had to fight the gender bias at every stage, which challenged them from moving forward. During her time, she had two research publications with Prof SP Chakravarthi and one with SK Chatterjee, who was an MSc in Applied Physics from Calcutta University and who had joined the Institute in 1946 as a lecturer in the Department of Electrical Technology.

Rajeshwari often wondered about this experience, "I am not sure whether I am progressing forward in my research career, or I am waiting to go abroad to get better qualified in the upcoming field of Electronics and ECE." Rajeshwari Chaterjee knew that to further her ground and hold on to the subject of science, she would have to pursue higher studies. This is when she started exploring abroad for a doctorate degree in science.

India was also undergoing change after the Second World War. Between 1945 and 1947, significant efforts were being made by the interim government in Delhi to promote the pursuit of science in India. Recognizing the importance of scientific research and education for the country's development, a scientific committee comprising eminent scientists such as Meghnad Saha, SS Bhatnagar, JC Ghosh, KS Krishnan, and Homi Bhabha was established. This committee played a crucial role in advocating for the initiation of a scholarship programme that was aimed at supporting talented Indian students in the fields of science and engineering. The programme's goal was to provide opportunities for research and higher education in leading academic institutions abroad, which included universities in the United States, Britain, and Canada. It was evident that for India to grow and sustain on its own terms, it was important to educate its bright youth for a brighter future.

Rajeshwari applied for one such scholarship that was being promoted back then, in the field of electronics and its applications. In 1946, Rajeshwari Chatterjee secured this prestigious scholarship, marking a noteworthy milestone in her academic journey. With her admission to the Department of Electrical Engineering at the University of Michigan, Ann Arbor, USA, she embarked on a transformative educational experience. Despite the challenges and societal norms of the time, which made it rare for women to travel abroad for studies, Rajeshwari demonstrated remarkable courage and determination. After months and years of struggle as a scientist, she felt that she would leave India to go to a more advanced country to learn something different, for better or for worse! However, there was still time for her actual travel to materialize. In those days, travelling to a foreign land, that too for a single female, was not the easiest of experiences. Tying up with streamers would take months to materialize, and travel by air was not that safe. After getting admission, it was a long wait for Rajeshwari to figure out the coordination for sailing.

It took several months for the interim Indian Government in Delhi to arrange her travel to the USA in the converted troop ship SS Marine Adder from Bombay (Mumbai) to San Francisco, USA, which left Bombay at the end of June 1947. Rajeshwari was nervous about this next chapter of her life, but she knew that this was a dream come true for her. She was not sure if the experience of a 25-year-old female would be enough to prepare her for an unknown higher education in the USA. But once she was on the boat travelling to the USA, she thoroughly enjoyed the trip and made a number of friends, many of them Indian students who were travelling to the USA for higher studies in different subjects and were from different parts of India. It was a learning experience, as the travel itself was long and there was not much to do on the ship. On the way, they also touched the ports of Singapore, Hong Kong, and Shanghai.

After about a month of travel in the Indian Ocean and the Pacific Ocean, the ship finally reached San Francisco at the end of July 1947. Even in the unknown land, they felt welcomed and supported. Though everything was still getting organized after World War II, the Education Secretary at the Indian Embassy in Washington, D.C., met the students at the docks in San Francisco and made arrangements for them to go to their respective universities in the USA or Canada.

Eventually, after a few months, Rajeshwari joined the Department of Electrical Engineering as a graduate (post-graduate) student. She was associated with her first adviser, Professor LN Holland, who guided her to take three undergraduate courses in the Fall semester before starting her graduate courses. As most of Rajeshwari's previous degrees were in physics and mathematics, she did not have an undergraduate degree in Electrical Engineering. These courses helped her to catch up on theoretical knowledge in the subject, which would then help her in her PhD. She completed her master's in Science in Engineering by the end of January. Rajeshwari did very well in these courses, as she knew that once she had a thorough understanding, she could take post-graduate courses on electron tubes, microwave engineering, and other subjects for her PhD.

Learning so much was an eye-opening experience for her, and she wanted to continue her work to obtain a PhD degree by specializing in electronics and vacuum tubes. However, the Government of India wanted her to move beyond learning theoretical subjects and to take some practical training before returning to India after two years in the USA. After all, the scholarship and support were meant for her to come back to contribute to India's growing technological needs.

While she waited for her future directions on her PhD, Rajeshwari decided to take an eight-month practical training in radio frequency measurements at the National Bureau of Standards in Washington, D.C., from February 1949 to mid-September 1949. In the meantime, she also applied for the Barbour Scholarship at the University of Michigan to continue her PhD degree. This was a full-tuition scholarship for high-achieving women with the most potential to give back to their home countries. She was lucky to be given the scholarship; thus, she requested the Government of India to give her permission to accept it. She knew her responsibilities towards her country and wanted to fully comply with the trust that had been shown in her. The Government of India accepted the request on the condition that she would come back to serve the country for three years and support in nation-building.

She worked on her PhD under Professor William Gould Dow, who was a very well-known scientist and professor at the University of Michigan. He had worked at length on microwave magnetrons in the

Radiation Laboratories at Massachusetts Institute of Technology (MIT) at Cambridge, and held a practical understanding of the topic. He was a pioneer in Electrical Engineering and had helped in developing life-saving radar jamming technology during the war. Professor Dow asked Rajeshwari to take some more courses on microwave vacuum tubes and allied subjects. Rajeshwari started enjoying the study of microwaves and was able to secure good grades in all these courses. On diving deep into the topic, she selected a research problem on vacuum tube trigger circuits, which is the basic circuit that was used in those days in vacuum tube computers.

Her decision to pursue higher education abroad underscored her commitment to academic excellence and her willingness to overcome obstacles in pursuit of her educational and professional goals. During her time at the University of Michigan, Rajeshwari's intellect, dedication, and passion for engineering shone brightly. She immersed herself in her research, thus exploring new frontiers in the field of Electrical Engineering with a keen focus on microwave technology.

Despite the challenges she faced as a woman studying in a predominantly male-dominated field, Rajeshwari remained undeterred in her pursuit of knowledge and excellence. Her determination and perseverance propelled her forward, thereby enabling her to overcome obstacles and excel in her doctoral studies. Rajeshwari's PhD experience in the United States not only enriched her academic and professional development but also played a pivotal role in shaping her future contributions to the field of engineering in India. Her accomplishments abroad served as a testament to her intellect, determination, and commitment to advancing the frontiers of science and engineering.

In 1953, after several years of rigorous research and academic pursuit, Rajeshwari successfully completed her PhD and obtained her doctoral degree from the University of Michigan. Prof Dow counselled

Rajeswari as she was quite stressed about the oral examination and completing her research thesis. An internal committee at Michigan reviewed her research and granted her the degree. Armed with her newfound expertise and knowledge, she returned to India to embark on a remarkable career as a pioneering engineer, educator, and researcher. The Government of India had booked her return via the UK, so she was able to spend some time sightseeing in London.

Finally, after five and a half years in the US, Rajeshwari arrived in Bombay on 2 April 1954. Coming back home was a mixed feeling for her. While on one hand, she had gathered so much from the US, on the other hand, she was uncertain about the opportunities that lay ahead for her. When she had left India a month before Independence on a British-Indian passport, India was in the middle of riots and partition struggles. It had affected everyone in many different ways, especially her friends and colleagues who belonged to areas that faced massive pushback. On arriving back, she made her way home to Karnataka as she had been away from her family for a long time. As the region had not suffered from any major issues because of independence and partition, she was also not worried.

Since she was coming back home after a long time, she knew that the question of her marriage would also be discussed. She, too, was keen to settle down, but was certain about marrying only a like-minded person who respected her work and, most importantly, valued the space that women could hold in the field of science. The year of her return, Rajeshwari married Sisir Kumar Chatterjee, who was a faculty member at IISc and with whom she had worked during her research stint at the institute.

Soon it was time for Rajeswari to think about the next chapter of her life in India. She learnt that the Government of India was considering her for a lecturer position in ECE at the Roorkee Engineering

College in Roorkee, UP. She also learned about an opportunity for a lectureship at the Indian Institute of Science in Bangalore. This was in the Department of ECE and was also the institute where her husband was newly appointed as an Assistant Professor. Given the convenience and prior positive experience at IISc, Rajeswari chose to apply for the same. Rajeswari Chatterjee became the first female faculty member of the esteemed Indian Institute of Science and began a new branch of her research career at the IISc.

Rajeswari happily joined as a lecturer in the ECE department in August 1953. As she came with rich subject matter experience, she was asked to teach Electromagnetic Theory to the final year students of the diploma course. The class of about 20 students had only one girl named Jaya, and the rest were boys. Given that it was a fresh course and subject, Rajeswari dived into giving all help to the students to excel in their course. The whole batch was inquisitive and went on to produce some well-known names in the field, like BS Atal and OP Gandhi.

After a few years, the course was converted into a BE degree, and ME courses were started in Advanced Electronics and Microwave Engineering. During this period, Rajeswari continued teaching in special fields such as Electromagnetic Theory, Microwave Engineering, and Antennas. She also came up with several papers and books on the topics. Her husband, Prof SK Chatterjee, also taught and guided research students in many courses on common subjects as well as on many other subjects like satellite communications and so on.

During the 1960s, Rajeswari and her husband introduced courses in microwave technology and satellite communication at IISc, further cementing the institution's reputation as a leader in engineering education and research in India. Recognizing the importance of hands-on experimentation and research infrastructure, they thought of initiating a lab for more experiential learning by students.

Rajeswari, along with her husband, initiated teaching and research in the area of microwave engineering for the first time in India. This was a big contribution that she and her husband were making in building the future of India. Rajeswari Chatterjee, along with her husband played a pivotal role in establishing the Microwave Engineering Research Laboratory at the Indian Institute of Science (IISc) in Bangalore. This endeavour marked a significant milestone in the advancement of engineering research in India, particularly in the field of microwave technology. Despite limited resources and funding, they demonstrated remarkable ingenuity and determination in building the necessary equipment and facilities for their research activities.

The microwave laboratory at IISc became a hub for pioneering research in microwave technology, thus attracting students, researchers, and scholars from across India and beyond. Rajeswari's expertise and leadership in the field, coupled with her husband's contributions, played a crucial role in shaping the laboratory into a centre of excellence for microwave research. There were always more female students in the microwave research lab, perhaps because both the Chatterjees felt that female students were more sincere and worked harder. For Rajeswari, her husband was a great support. They were both deeply passionate and driven by their work and led simple lives.

Rajeswari went on to become a professor and also held the position of Chairman in the Department of ECE. Besides teaching electromagnetic theory, electron tube circuits, and microwave technology, she was also very active in research. She received numerous awards and recognition for her work in research and science. She formally retired from the position at the age of sixty in 1992, but she didn't quit science. SK Chatterjee died in 1994, but Rajeshwari continued to lead an active life.

Rajeshwari Chatterjee continued to mentor students and also worked on social programmes with the Indian Association for Women's

Studies, thus promoting the education of women in the field of science and technology. She went on to write a book about the plight of women as professionals. In her book, she elaborated on her own journey, but also on the many families where women were not allowed to keep the money that they earned for themselves. She worked on addressing many issues of caste segregation, gender discrimination, and financial instability. Rajeshwari knew the importance of mentorship, which she provided to many during and after her formal career. She wrote more than a hundred and ten papers and seven books in the field of science and societal issues.

Even in the last few days of her life, Rajeswari was active and often visited her daughter, Indira Chatterjee, a Professor of Electrical and Biomedical Engineering at the University of Nevada, Reno, USA. Rajeswari passed away on 3 September 2010 in India.

Throughout her life, Rajeshwari received recognition for her contributions and work in the field. She received the Mountbatten Prize from the Institute of Electrical and Radio Engineering (UK) for the best paper. Then she also received the JC Bose Memorial Prize by the Institution of Engineers for the best research paper. Recently, Chatterjee was granted a posthumous honour, as one of the 'first women achievers of India' by the Union Ministry of Women and Child Development.

More than 30 years of her contribution to building the department at IISc and carrying out pioneering research in the field of microwave and antenna technology will always be remembered. She led an inspiring life that left a huge imprint on the lives of many women scientists and engineers in India.

6.

Kalpana Chawla

Kalpana Chawla was the first woman of Indian origin to fly into space. She was an American Astronaut and an Aerospace Engineer.

India's science and technological advancement story is not an easy one. On one hand, where the struggle for independence was real, on the other hand, India had to shape and figure out the path for its development. While the governments have always been futuristic and aimed to identify and invest in opportunities, the story of Indian society was slow-paced.

Kalpana Chawla was born on 17 March 1962, into a loving middle-class family in Karnal, Haryana, India. Her parents were Banarasi Lal Chawla and Sanjyothi Chawla. They were supportive of Kalpana and her siblings by fostering an environment where education and personal growth were encouraged. She was the youngest of four siblings. Her two elder sisters, Sunita and Deepa, along with her elder brother Sanjay, were all supportive of Kalpana and her aspirations. From a young age, Kalpana showed an interest in flying and space, often staring at the sky and dreaming of exploring beyond the Earth. Her entire family played a significant role in shaping her character and values. Their encouragement and belief in her abilities instilled in Kalpana the confidence to pursue her passion for aviation and space exploration.

In her childhood, Kalpana Chawla was known by a special nickname—Montu. But when she was three years old, she chose the name Kalpana for herself. Kalpana, which means 'idea' or 'imagination' in Hindi, always possessed a vibrant imagination. From a tender age, she was drawn to the mysteries of the universe, often gazing up at the stars and dreaming of adventures beyond the Earth's atmosphere. When the time came for Kalpana to start school, she was filled with excitement and anticipation.

Her early education took place in Karnal, where she attended the Tagore Baal Niketan School. This laid the groundwork for her academic pursuits. She excelled in her studies by demonstrating a natural aptitude for mathematics and science. Her teachers recognized her talent and dedication, which fuelled her ambition to pursue a career in Aeronautical Engineering.

Despite the societal norms of the time that discouraged girls from pursuing careers in fields like science and engineering, Kalpana was determined to follow her passion for aviation. From a young age, Kalpana displayed a keen interest in the mysteries of the universe. She would often gaze at the night sky, captivated by the stars, and dream of exploring space. This fascination with flight and space exploration became the driving force in her life. Her fascination with flight and aircraft was fostered by her father's passion for aviation. As a child, she would often accompany her father to local flying clubs, where they would watch planes take off and land. These outings sparked Kalpana's imagination and further ignited her interest in the wonders of aviation.

Accompanying her father to the flying clubs provided Kalpana with firsthand exposure to the world of aviation. Watching the planes soar through the sky filled her with a sense of wonder and awe, thus inspiring her to dream of one day taking flight herself. These experiences planted the seeds of Kalpana's lifelong passion for aviation and space exploration. They laid the foundation for her future endeavours as an Aeronautical Engineer and astronaut, thus shaping her determination to pursue her dreams of reaching the stars.

Kalpana Chawla's journey towards further education faced initial challenges and setbacks, as she encountered barriers due to societal expectations and gender biases. Her aspiration to become an Aeronautical Engineer was marked by determination and resilience in the face of familial and societal expectations. Despite her father's advice to pursue a more traditional career path, such as medicine or teaching, Kalpana remained steadfast in her desire to become a flight engineer. Her unwavering determination was met with resistance when she expressed her intention to pursue Aeronautical Engineering. She encountered scepticism from counsellors who warned her about limited job opportunities in the field within the country. However, Kalpana refused to be swayed by their concerns.

Despite her aspirations to pursue Aeronautical Engineering, she initially faced disappointment in her attempts to gain admission to prestigious institutions like IIT Delhi. Even when she didn't get accepted into IIT Delhi for both mechanical and chemical engineering, Kalpana's determination remained steadfast. She didn't allow these setbacks to deter her from her ultimate goal.

Instead, she seized the opportunity presented by Punjab Engineering College, which offered her a seat. However, even there, she encountered resistance due to the lack of female students in the aeronautics programme. Despite being the only girl to choose Aeronautical Engineering in the course selection process, Kalpana stood her ground. Her unwavering commitment to her dreams and her passion for flight engineering propelled her forward, undeterred by the obstacles in her path. Here, Kalpana's mother played a crucial role in supporting her daughter's aspirations by persuading her father to stand by Kalpana's decision. With her family's support, Kalpana pursued her chosen path with confidence and determination.

Despite being encouraged to consider other courses, Kalpana remained resolute in her decision to pursue Aeronautical Engineering. Her determination and passion for her chosen field soon transcended the gender divide, as she proved herself capable and deserving of her place in the programme. Kalpana enrolled at Punjab Engineering College, Chandigarh, India, where she pursued a Bachelor of Science degree in Aeronautical Engineering. Her academic excellence and dedication to her studies earned her a place among the top students in her class. She refused to be constrained by societal expectations or gender stereotypes, choosing instead to carve her path in a field that was traditionally dominated by men.

Kalpana Chawla's achievement in becoming the first woman Aeronautical Engineer to graduate from Punjab Engineering College (PEC) in 1982 was a testament to her exceptional abilities and dedication to her field. Kalpana knew that she would need to explore degrees abroad to be able to learn and grow further in her career, as infrastructure and education in India were not enough to support her dreams of flying high. Her outstanding academic and co-curricular performance paved the way for her admission into the master's course in Aerospace Engineering at the University of Texas in the United States. However, she did not receive full family support in pursuing her dreams. Despite familial resistance, Kalpana joined a master's degree abroad.

Like in the lives of many females, Kalpana's family too had concerns. They were concerned about her studying abroad and the potential impact this would have on her marriage and future family plans, which reflected the societal and cultural norms prevalent at the time, particularly regarding gender roles and expectations from women. However, Kalpana's unwavering commitment to her goals and her belief in the importance of education drove her to pursue her dreams despite these obstacles.

Her decision to pursue higher education abroad not only expanded her academic and professional horizons but also paved the way for her groundbreaking career as an Aerospace Engineer and Astronaut. Kalpana's journey is a powerful example of resilience, determination, and the importance of following one's passion, even in the face of familial resistance and societal expectations.

Kalpana Chawla's decision to immigrate to the United States in the 1980s to further her studies marked a significant chapter in her life. Becoming a naturalized citizen reflected her commitment to her academic and professional pursuits in the United States. This transition allowed her to access advanced educational opportunities and immerse herself in the vibrant Aerospace Engineering community in the US. Her success in gaining admission to such a prestigious programme further underscored her talent and determination. The opportunity to pursue advanced studies in Aerospace Engineering in the United States provided Kalpana with access to world-class resources, faculty, and research opportunities, thus allowing her to further expand her knowledge and skills in her chosen field.

Kalpana Chawla's academic journey in the United States was impressive. After completing her first master's degree in Aerospace Engineering at the University of Texas, she continued to pursue higher education at the University of Colorado Boulder. There, she earned a second master's degree in 1986 and went on to achieve a PhD in Aerospace Engineering in 1988. Her dedication to advancing her knowledge and expertise in Aerospace Engineering through multiple degrees underscores her commitment to her field. The University of Colorado Boulder provided her with an enriching academic environment and research opportunities that allowed her to excel in her studies and make significant contributions to the field.

Kalpana Chawla's PhD thesis, titled *'Computation of dynamics and control of unsteady vortical flows'*, reflects her deep engagement with complex aerodynamic phenomena and her focus on advancing the understanding and control of vortical flows. In her research, she delved into Computational Fluid Dynamics (CFD) techniques to model and analyze the behaviour of unsteady vortical flows that are characterized by the formation and interaction of vortices, which play a crucial role in aerodynamic phenomena such as lift generation, flow separation, and turbulence.

Chawla's work involved developing computational models and algorithms to simulate the dynamics of vortical flows under various conditions. By gaining insights into the behaviour of these flows, she explored strategies for controlling or mitigating their effects, which could have implications for aircraft performance, stability, and safety.

Her thesis topic suggests a focus on both theoretical understanding and practical applications, thereby reflecting her interdisciplinary approach to Aerospace Engineering research. Through her doctoral work, Chawla made significant contributions to the field of aerodynamics by laying the groundwork for advancements in aircraft design, control systems, and simulations in fluid dynamics.

With her eyes fixed on the sky and her heart yearning for adventure, Kalpana Chawla crossed paths with Jean Pierre Harrison, a flying instructor and aviation author whose passion for flight rivalled her own. From the moment they met, a spark ignited between them with a shared love for the boundless freedom of the skies. Under Jean Pierre's guidance, Kalpana's journey into the world of piloting began, which would take her to heights she never dared to imagine. Kalpana and Jean went on to get married on 02 December 1983.

With unwavering commitment and unyielding dedication, Kalpana immersed herself in the art of flight. She soared through the skies, mastering the controls of aeroplanes, gliders, and myriad aircraft with grace and precision. With each passing day, her skills as a pilot grew stronger, while her passion burned brighter than ever before. Kalpana's determination knew no bounds. She pursued her dreams with relentless fervour, earning licences for single and multi-engine aeroplanes, seaplanes, and gliders. Her thirst for knowledge was unquenchable, her hunger for adventure insatiable.

But Kalpana's journey was not just about conquering the skies; it was about sharing her passion with others. Armed with her certification as a Flight Instructor, she became a beacon of inspiration for aspiring pilots around the world. Her wisdom, her guidance, and her unwavering belief in the power of flight touched the lives of all those who had the privilege of learning from her.

In 1988, soon after completing her PhD, Kalpana joined NASA's Ames Research Centre. Kalpana Chawla's tenure at the research centre marked the beginning of her illustrious career with the space agency. Her initial focus on CFD research, specifically on Vertical and Short Take-Off and Landing (V/STOL) concepts, highlights her dedication to advancing aerospace technology and aircraft design.

At NASA Ames, Chawla's research contributions were significant and far-reaching, as evidenced by her work that was published in technical journals and conference papers. Her expertise in CFD enabled her to investigate and analyze the complex aerodynamic phenomena involved in power-lift aircraft, which are crucial for vertical or short take-off and landing operations.

Kalpana Chawla's research output, which included her work in CFD and Aerodynamics, came to be widely recognized and respected within the scientific community. Many of her findings and insights have been documented in technical journals and presented at prestigious conferences. The publication of research findings in technical journals is an essential aspect of academic and scientific learning that she fostered during her time at the research centre. It allowed Kalpana to share the discoveries, methodologies, and innovations with her peers, thus facilitating collaborations, validations, and further advancements in the field. By presenting her work at conferences, Chawla had the opportunity to engage with fellow researchers, receive feedback, and showcase her contributions to the field of Aerospace Engineering.

Kalpana Chawla's desire to take her research further and engage in real-time experiments meant that she was looking at her ambition and dedication to push the boundaries of Aerospace Engineering. Transitioning from computational simulations to real-world experimentation is a natural progression for researchers who seek to validate their findings and explore new frontiers in their field. At NASA's Ames Research Centre, Chawla had access to state-of-the-art facilities and resources that enabled her to conduct real-time experiments and test the practical applications of her research. Whether it involved wind tunnel testing, flight testing, or other experimental methods, engaging in real-world experiments provided Chawla with valuable insights and data to further enhance her understanding of aerodynamics and flight dynamics.

By contemplating her next steps at NASA's Ames Research Centre, Kalpana started thinking about advancing her research and contributing to the broader goals of space exploration and Aerospace Engineering. Her willingness to explore new avenues and pursue challenges speaks of her adventurous spirit and determination to make meaningful contributions in her field.

Kalpana embarked on a new adventure in 1993 by joining Overset Methods Inc. as Vice President and Research Scientist. At Overset Methods Inc., Kalpana found herself surrounded by a team of brilliant minds, all dedicated to unravelling the mysteries of moving multiple body problems. Together, they embarked on a journey to push the boundaries of aerospace simulations, hence seeking to unlock new insights into the dynamic systems in motion. As a key member of the team, Kalpana took on the monumental task of spearheading the development and implementation of efficient techniques for aerodynamic optimization. With her keen intellect and unwavering determination, she dove headfirst into the challenge, determined to pave the way for groundbreaking advancements in the field.

After becoming a naturalized US citizen in April 1991, she wasted no time in pursuing her next challenge: applying for the NASA Astronaut Corps. In 1994, Kalpana's aspirations took flight as she was selected as an astronaut candidate, marking the beginning of an intensive year of training and preparation. She immersed herself in the rigorous demands of astronaut training, thereby honing her skills and preparing herself for the challenges that lay ahead.

As a crew representative for the Astronaut Office EVA/Robotics and Computer Branches, Kalpana's expertise in engineering and technology proved invaluable. She worked tirelessly with Robotic Situational Awareness Displays and tested software for the space shuttles, thus gaining hands-on experience that would serve her well in the years to come.

In March 1995, Kalpana officially joined the prestigious ranks of the NASA Astronaut Corps, a milestone that marked the culmination of years of hard work and dedication. Her selection for her first flight in 1997 was a testament to her exceptional abilities and readiness to take on the challenges of space exploration.

Kalpana Chawla's historic journey into space aboard the Space Shuttle Columbia on 19 November 1997 marked a monumental milestone not only for her but also for India and the global community. As part of the six-astronaut crew of the STS-87 mission, Kalpana blazed a trail as the first Indian woman to venture into the cosmos.

The mission was not just a journey of personal achievement but also a voyage of scientific discovery. On STS-87, Kalpana and her fellow astronauts embarked on a series of experiments designed to unravel the mysteries of how the weightless space environment affects various physical processes. From studying the behaviour of fluids and flames to exploring the intricacies of materials science, their work promised to deepen our understanding of the universe and pave the way for future space explorations.

Over the course of the mission, the Space Shuttle Columbia orbited the Earth an astonishing 252 times, covering a distance of 6.5 million miles. For 376 hours and 34 minutes, Kalpana and her crewmates marvelled at the beauty of our planet from the vantage point of space, while conducting experiments, conducting repairs, and navigating the challenges of life in microgravity.

Kalpana Chawla's role as the mission specialist and prime robotic arm operator on the Space Shuttle Columbia flight STS-87 brought her to the forefront of scientific exploration in space. Alongside her fellow astronauts, Kevin Kregel, Steven Linsey, Winston Scott, Takao Doi, and Leonid Kadenyuk, Kalpana embarked on a mission that was filled with groundbreaking experiments and ambitious objectives.

During the STS-87 mission, the crew conducted a variety of experiments aimed at studying plant reproduction in microgravity and investigating how materials behave in the unique space environment. These experiments held the promise of unlocking new insights into fundamental biological and physical processes, with implications for both space exploration and life on Earth. One of the most significant tasks entrusted to Kalpana during the mission was the deployment of a satellite called SPARTAN 201 using the robotic arm. The satellite was designed to study the outer layer of the sun, known as the corona. However, a malfunction prevented the satellite from controlling its position upon deployment, thus prompting a challenging situation for the crew.

In a remarkable display of teamwork and ingenuity, two of Kalpana's fellow astronauts performed a spacewalk to recapture the malfunctioning satellite, preventing it from drifting aimlessly in space. Though the SPARTAN 201 mission did not go as planned, the crew's swift response and decisive action demonstrated their resilience and adaptability in the face of adversity.

Reflecting on her experiences during the mission, Kalpana Chawla beautifully captured the profound sense of interconnectedness that space exploration evoked. She eloquently expressed, "When you look at the stars and the galaxy, you feel that you are not just from any particular piece of land, but from the solar system." Her words resonate with the awe-inspiring wonder of the cosmos and the shared humanity that unites us all in our quest for knowledge and understanding.

Following the successful completion of the STS-87 mission and its post-flight activities, Kalpana Chawla's journey as an astronaut continued to evolve. Recognized for her expertise, dedication, and contributions to space exploration, she was assigned to technical positions within the astronaut office, where she played a crucial role in shaping the future of human space flight.

In her new role, Chawla focused her efforts on advancing the development and operations of the International Space Station (ISS). As one of the most ambitious projects in the history of space exploration, the ISS represented a monumental achievement in international collaboration and scientific research.

Drawing on her extensive background in Aerospace Engineering and her firsthand experience as an astronaut, Chawla contributed her expertise to a wide range of technical challenges and operational considerations that were related to the ISS. From designing and testing new systems and equipment to developing protocols for crew training and mission planning, her work was instrumental in ensuring the success of the space station programmes.

Chawla's dedication to her work and her unwavering commitment to excellence made her a valuable asset to the astronaut office and the broader space community. Her contributions helped to pave the way for continued expansion and utilization of the ISS as a platform for scientific research, technological innovation, and international cooperation.

Kalpana Chawla's selection for her second voyage into space, as a Mission Specialist on STS-107 on Space Shuttle Columbia, marked another significant chapter in her illustrious career as an astronaut. The mission, which faced several delays, was finally launched on 16 January 2003, with Chawla and her crewmates embarking on a 16-day journey of scientific exploration.

During the STS-107 mission, Kalpana Chawla played a pivotal role in overseeing and conducting a diverse array of scientific experiments, each aimed at unlocking new insights into the fundamental processes of life and the universe in the unique environment of microgravity.

One of the key areas of focus for Chawla and her fellow astronauts was crystal growth, a process that is greatly affected by the absence of gravity. By studying how crystals form and grow in space, scientists hoped to gain a better understanding of their properties and potential applications in the fields of medicine, materials science, and electronics.

In addition to crystal growth experiments, Chawla and the STS-107 crew conducted research into combustion and fire suppression in space. Understanding how fire behaves in microgravity was essential for ensuring the safety of astronauts and spacecraft during long-duration missions, as well as for developing more effective fire suppression systems for use in space. Another notable aspect of the STS-107 mission was its focus on biomedical research, which included studies related to prostate cancer. Chawla's involvement in these experiments underscored her commitment to advancing scientific knowledge and exploring the potential applications of space research in improving human health and well-being.

Throughout the sixteen-day mission, Chawla and her crewmates performed over 80 scientific experiments, each contributing to our understanding of the universe and our place within it. Their dedication, expertise, and tireless efforts in the pursuit of scientific discovery exemplified their spirit of exploration and collaboration that defines human spaceflight.

However, there was an unfortunate end to all this, which no one had foreseen. During the launch of the STS-107 mission, tragedy struck when a piece of foam insulation broke off from the space shuttle's external tank and struck the port wing of the orbiter, Columbia. This event occurred on 16 January 2003, just moments after liftoff, during the ascent phase of the mission.

Foam shedding during shuttle launches is not uncommon, and as a result, previous missions had experienced minor damage. However, in the case of STS-107, some engineers and analysts grew concerned that the damage to Columbia's wing might be more severe than initially thought. The foam strike was captured by cameras and reviewed by engineers on the ground. Analysis of the footage raised concerns about the potential for damage to the Thermal Protection System (TPS) on the wing, which was crucial for protecting the orbiter during re-entry into the Earth's atmosphere. Despite these concerns, the severity of the damage was not fully understood or appreciated at the time. In the absence of clear evidence indicating a significant threat to the safety of the mission, the decision was made to proceed with the flight as planned.

The morning of 01 February 2003 marks a tragic day in the history of space exploration as the Space Shuttle Columbia, returning from its

STS-107 mission, encountered a catastrophic failure during re-entry into the Earth's atmosphere.

As the shuttle re-entered the atmosphere, travelling at immense speed, hot gases began to penetrate the damaged area of the orbiter's wing, where a briefcase-sized piece of insulation had broken off during launch and damaged the S. This critical shield, designed to protect the shuttle from the intense heat that is generated during re-entry, had been compromised, thus leading to the unfolding tragedy. The instability caused by the compromised TPS resulted in the shuttle rolling and bucking, subjecting the crew to violent forces and chaos within the cabin. In less than a minute, the shuttle depressurized, sealing the fate of the crew.

Tragically, all seven astronauts aboard the Columbia were lost as the shuttle broke up over Texas and Louisiana before plunging into the ground. The loss of the entire crew, Rick D Husband, William C McCool, Michael P Anderson, Ilan Ramon, Kalpana Chawla, David M Brown, and Laurel B Clark, sent shockwaves through NASA and the global space community, mourning the loss of courageous explorers and dedicated scientists.

The Columbia disaster was the second major tragedy to strike the space shuttle programme, following the loss of the space shuttle Challenger in 1986. It served as a sombre reminder of the inherent risks of space exploration and the importance of constant vigilance, thorough risk assessments, and safety protocols to ensure the well-being of astronauts and the success of missions. In the aftermath of the Columbia disaster, NASA undertook a comprehensive investigation to determine the causes of the accident and implemented significant changes to improve the safety and reliability of future space shuttle missions. The legacy of the Columbia crew lives on as a testament to their courage, dedication, and sacrifice in the pursuit of knowledge and exploration beyond the bounds of the Earth.

While Kalpana went down early at the age of 40, she left many lessons and motivations for young girls to dream. From 1998, every year her school in Karnal sent two girls to the Foundation for International Space Education's United Space School in Houston, and Chawla would invite them into her home for an Indian dinner. She received many awards and recognition for her contributions to the field of science and aeronautics.

The University of Texas dedicated a Kalpana Chawla memorial at the Arlington College of Engineering in 2010. At the time of its opening, the display included a flight suit, photographs, information about Chawla's life, and a flag that was flown over the Johnson Space Centre during a memorial for the Columbia astronauts.

In October 2020, a commercial cargo spacecraft named after Chawla launched to the ISS. Northrop Grumman's Cygnus capsule was named the SS Kalpana Chawla, as it is the company's policy to dedicate its Cygnus capsules to someone who has played a pivotal role in human spaceflight. Kalpana was posthumously awarded the Congressional Space Medal of Honour, the NASA Space Flight Medal, and the NASA Distinguished Service Medal.

Kalpana spoke the following words while travelling in the weightlessness of space, "You are just your intelligence". She had travelled 10.67 million km, as many as 252 times around the Earth. She led a life that started with several challenges, but she continued to follow the dreams she had seen at a very young age. She left this world a much better place than she found it.

7.

Aditi Pant

Aditi Pant, an Indian Oceanographer, was the first Indian woman to visit Antarctica. She held prominent positions at various institutions, including the National Institute of Oceanography, National Chemical Laboratory, University of Pune, and Maharashtra Academy of Sciences.

In the early nineties, general education systems in India were very constrained not only in terms of gender and geography but also topically. In the past, only a few had ventured into fields that were not common. This was even more true for women as they were not encouraged to explore. One such field was oceanography. In India, there were very few research institutions and far less advancement in technology. While globally, the momentum was picking up, within the country, there were very few collaborations.

In India, one name that shines bright in the history of oceanography is that of Aditi Pant. Her upbringing in a family with a strong academic and diplomatic background played a significant role in shaping her interest in science and exploration. Born into a Marathi-speaking Deshastha Brahmin family in Nagpur on 05 July 1943, she was surrounded by intellectual stimulation and a culture of excellence from an early age. Her father, Appa Saheb Pant, served the Government of India for 40 years as a respected diplomat, holding positions such as High Commissioner in various countries across Europe and Africa. His experiences and exposure to diverse cultures instilled in Aditi a sense of curiosity about the world and its interconnectedness. Aditi's mother, Nalini Devi, added to the intellectual environment of their household as a medical doctor and a Fellow of the Royal College of Surgeons. Growing up in a family where both parents were accomplished in their respective fields fostered an environment of academic curiosity and encouraged Aditi to pursue her interests in science.

From a young age, Aditi showed a keen interest in science, a passion that was nurtured by her family's encouragement and support. Her upbringing in a family that valued education and intellectual pursuits provided her with the foundation to excel in her academic and professional endeavours. The combination of her family's influence, her own natural curiosity, and her early exposure to the world of science set Aditi on a path towards a distinguished career in oceanography and scientific exploration.

Aditi's early experiences in the kitchen, under the guidance of her mother, laid the foundation for her career in science in unexpected ways. While learning to cook rice, dal, and potatoes at the age of ten, Aditi was taught not just the recipes but the importance of consistency, attention to detail, and precision in measurements. Her mother's insistence on achieving consistent results reflected a deeper philosophy about the importance of paying attention, knowing what one is doing, and measuring things correctly. These principles, although initially applied in the context of cooking, resonated with Aditi and became ingrained in her approach to problem-solving and in understanding the world around her.

Despite struggling to keep pace with her racing mind and achieving only 'somewhat edible' results in the kitchen, Aditi's experiences taught her valuable lessons about observation, pattern recognition, and the importance of methodical thinking. While she may have been 'hopeless' at practical chemistry and biology, she found solace in her ability to discern patterns and visualize abstract concepts in her mind. This innate ability to see the 'pattern of things' proved to be a valuable asset in her scientific pursuits. It allowed her to approach complex problems with a unique perspective, thus enabling her to make connections and draw insights that others overlooked. While Aditi's culinary skills may not have been her forte, her early experiences in the kitchen instilled in her a mindset of curiosity, perseverance, and attention to detail that served her well throughout her career in science. They taught her the importance of consistency, precision, and the value of learning from both successes and failures.

Aditi Pant's childhood was marked by diligence, sincerity in her studies, and a deep love for outdoor activities. Raised in an intellectually stimulating environment, she was inspired by her father, Appa Saheb Pant, whose diplomatic career and broad interests sparked her curiosity about the world. Their dinner conversations, ranging from engines to stars, provided Aditi with a wealth of knowledge and fuelled her interest in science and exploration. These discussions not only expanded her horizons but also instilled in her a sense of wonder and a thirst for knowledge.

Aditi's love for outdoor activities, such as hiking and trekking, which she shared with her father, became a source of inspiration and a reflection of her desire for freedom, which further fuelled her longing for a career that would allow her both mental freedom and the opportunity to explore the world around her. She yearned for a profession that would enable her to move freely and engage with the natural environment. Hiking and trekking provided Aditi with a sense of liberation and a connection to the natural world. They allowed her to break free from the constraints of everyday life, to immerse herself in the beauty of nature, and to experience a sense of personal growth and self-discovery.

This upbringing shaped Aditi's aspirations and set her on a path towards a career in oceanography. Her desire for intellectual freedom and a sense of adventure found resonance in the field of scientific explorations, where she could combine her passion for learning with her love for the outdoors. Ultimately, Aditi Pant's childhood experiences, her family's influence, and her innate curiosity laid the foundation for her remarkable journey as a pioneering Oceanographer and Adventurer.

For Aditi, the allure of a career that offered freedom of movement was not merely about physical mobility but also about intellectual and creative freedom. She sought a profession that would enable her to explore new horizons, to push the boundaries of knowledge, and to pursue her passions with a sense of autonomy and independence.

As Aditi Pant grew up and nurtured her passion for science and exploration, she pursued her higher education at the University of Pune. In 1964, she opted for a Bachelor of Science (BSc) degree and embarked on a journey of academic discovery, immersing herself in the study of various scientific disciplines. The University of Pune, renowned for its academic excellence and research opportunities, provided Aditi with a rich and stimulating learning environment. Here, she had access to top-notch faculty, state-of-the-art laboratories, and a diverse community of scholars and students. During her time at the university, Aditi delved into the fundamentals of science, thus gaining a comprehensive understanding of physics, chemistry, biology, and mathematics. Her coursework equipped her with the knowledge and skills that were necessary to pursue a career in a scientific field of her choice. Additionally, the University of Pune offered opportunities for hands-on research and practical training, thereby allowing Aditi to apply theoretical concepts to real-world problems and gain valuable experience in scientific inquiry and experimentation.

As Aditi Pant was completing her Bachelor of Science degree at the University of Pune, a pivotal moment occurred that shaped her future career path. A friend of her father's gifted her a book titled *The Open*

Sea by Sir Alister Hardy, a renowned Cambridge biologist. This book provided fascinating insights into the intricate and captivating world of plankton, as observed by Hardy during his research expeditions. For Aditi, *The Open Sea* served as a window into the vast and mysterious realm of the oceans. Through Hardy's vivid descriptions and scientific observations, she gained a deeper understanding of the complexities of marine life and the interconnectedness of oceanic ecosystems.

The book sparked a profound interest and curiosity in Aditi, thus igniting a passion for oceanography that shaped her future endeavours. She was captivated by the beauty and diversity of marine organisms, as well as the ecological dynamics that governed life in the open sea. From that moment, Aditi was hooked. She delved deeper into the study of oceanography, devouring books, conducting research, and seeking opportunities to learn more about this fascinating field. Her allure with the oceans and their inhabitants became a driving force in her academic and professional pursuits. The book not only inspired Aditi to pursue a career in oceanography but also instilled in her a sense of wonder and reverence for the natural world. It was a transformative experience that set her on a path of scientific explorations and discoveries, as she unravelled the mysteries of the oceans and contributed to our understanding of this vital and complex ecosystem.

Aditi's passion for oceanography drove her to seek opportunities abroad, knowing that Indian universities might not offer the comprehensive education and resources that she needed in this field. However, she faced the challenge of financial constraints within her family, which meant that scholarships were her only ticket to pursuing her dreams.

Receiving the US Government scholarship to study at the University of Hawaii was a moment of immense joy and triumph for Aditi. It not only validated her academic achievements and potential but also provided her with the means to pursue her passion without the burden of financial worries. The University of Hawaii, which was renowned for its well-known programmes in oceanography and marine sciences, offered Aditi the opportunity to immerse herself in a world-class academic environment and engage with leading experts in the field. It was a dream come true for Aditi, who eagerly embraced the chance to expand her knowledge, conduct research, and gain hands-on experience in Oceanographic studies.

This scholarship represented more than just a financial opportunity for Aditi; it was a gateway to a future that was filled with possibilities and opportunities for growth and advancement in her chosen field. It allowed her to pursue her passion for oceanography on an international stage, thereby paving the way for a successful and fulfilling career in scientific explorations and discoveries.

Aditi's Master of Science (MSc) thesis focused on the fascinating world of plankton, building upon her initial exposure to this subject through *The Open Sea.* As she delved deeper into the biology of the oceans, she became particularly intrigued by photosynthesis in plankton communities. Plankton, comprising a diverse array of organisms, play a crucial role in marine ecosystems. Some plankton photosynthesize, while others are grazers or secondary consumers. Bacteria play a vital role in recycling nutrients, thus contributing to the complex web of interactions within plankton communities.

Aditi's research aimed to investigate the effects of tropical light intensities on photosynthesis in natural plankton communities, as well as the flow of reduced carbon from phytoplankton to bacteria. However, she encountered challenges in directly calculating transfer rates in the sea. Collaborating with her guide, Dr MS Doty, they concluded that a single alga-single bacterium model was necessary before studying the entire plankton community. Fortuitously, Professor GE Fogg FRS of

Westfield College, London University, shared Aditi's perspective. With support from Professor Fogg, Aditi embarked on her research journey. Securing an MS degree, she underwent a rigorous examination at Westfield College, where Professor Fogg's offer to tour his lab signalled a significant opportunity.

Subsequently, Aditi obtained a SERC grant and a stipend for her studies, thus providing both financial stability and the means to pursue her research goals. With determination and support, she ventured into the world of scientific explorations, thereby paving the way for groundbreaking discoveries in oceanography. As Aditi completed her research and PhD, she was constantly thinking about what was next in her learning curve and career. Initially, she had her sights on two or three labs where she wanted to work, but little did she know that destiny had other plans for her.

Aditi's encounter with Professor NK Panikkar, a senior scientist with CSIR and founder-director of the National Institute of Oceanography (NIO) in Goa, proved to be a turning point in her career. During their discussions, the topic of job availability in India arose, which reflected the challenges faced by young professionals in the country during the early 1970s. The question of whether India truly valued its youth resonated deeply with Aditi and her peers, who grappled with the scarcity of job opportunities and the allure of better salaries abroad. However, Professor Panikkar's response left a lasting impression on Aditi. Despite acknowledging the challenges, he emphasized the abundance of untapped opportunities for those with the courage to seize them.

This conversation was a catalyst for Aditi's decision to return to India and pursue a career in oceanography. The prospect of meaningful work and the desire to contribute to her homeland outweighed the allure of higher salaries abroad or the disappointment her father might have felt if she chose to settle elsewhere. Moreover, Aditi felt a sense of responsibility to challenge the prevailing narrative about India's apathy towards its youth and to demonstrate that there were opportunities for those willing to pursue them. Her decision to forgo tenure positions and post-doctoral opportunities abroad in favour of a Pool Officer position in India reflected her commitment to embracing the challenges and opportunities that lay ahead in her home country.

Aditi's tenure at the NIO from 1973 to 1976 was marked by intensive field investigations along the Indian coastline, which were driven by the practical needs and constraints of their circumstances. During this period, she conducted comprehensive surveys and studies along the west coast of India, from Veraval to Kanyakumari, as well as in the region of the Gulf of Mannar. The NIO's focus on beachfront investigations encompassed a wide range of research topics, which included coastal ecology, marine biodiversity, sedimentology, and oceanography. These studies aimed to enhance our understanding of the coastal ecosystems and their importance for marine life, as well as to address pressing environmental and conservation issues.

Aditi's experiences during her fieldwork with NIO were marked by camaraderie, resourcefulness, and a sense of solidarity among the team members. Despite the challenges of limited accommodation and basic amenities, such as food and water, everyone worked together to accomplish their objectives. Sleeping on the beaches due to a lack of accommodation, the team made do with whatever resources were available to them, often relying on the local teashops for sustenance, which typically provided *bhajjias* (fritters) and jaggery tea. Despite the rustic conditions, Aditi recalls that she never worried about basic necessities like food, water, or privacy.

Being the only woman on the team, Aditi received special attention and care from the local villagers, particularly the women, who ensured that she had everything she needed, which included hot water for bathing in their huts. While her colleagues teased her about being a "woman scientist", they were secretly relieved that they didn't have to worry about her well-being. Aditi took advantage of her spare time to engage with the local women, using her basic Hindi skills to explain the purpose of their research in terms that resonated with their everyday experiences, such as fishing. This interaction not only fostered a deeper connection with the local community but also helped Aditi in appreciating the significance of their work and its impact on the lives of the people that they served. Overall, Aditi's fieldwork experiences taught her the value of teamwork, adaptability, and effective communication. Despite the challenging conditions, she found fulfilment in her work and forged meaningful connections with both her colleagues and the communities which they served.

In addition to their coastal research efforts, the NIO was also involved in a long-term programme in the Antarctic Ocean. This programme, spanning ten years, involved interdisciplinary studies on various topics that included the natural life-cycles of Antarctic organisms, material science related to polar environments, and other scientific disciplines. During this period, Aditi's work at the NIO provided her with valuable field experience and exposure to a diverse range of marine environments and research methodologies. It also contributed to the broader scientific understanding of the Indian coastal ecosystems and their significance in global oceanography.

Aditi Pant's expedition to Antarctica between December 1983 and March 1984 marked a significant milestone in India's scientific exploration of the continent. This expedition, part of the Indian Antarctic Programme initiated by Prime Minister Indira Gandhi, aimed to gather essential data on various aspects of the Antarctic environment, which included physics, chemistry, and biology. While driven by political considerations, it also had a significant scientific front. The expedition aimed to establish India's presence in Antarctica alongside other global powers. However, it was also a crucial opportunity for scientific explorations and research.

The Third expedition to Antarctica in 1983-1984, led by the National Centre for Antarctic and Ocean Research (NCAOR), included a diverse team of 83 members. Among them were two women scientists, Marine Biologist Dr Aditi Pant and Structural Geologist Prof Sudipta Sengupta. This expedition represented a significant milestone in India's scientific exploration of Antarctica. The Antarctic represents a dream for scientists, a pristine environment that is rich with opportunities to uncover valuable insights into the Earth's history and climate. Some members of the expedition focused on studying ice core samples and conducting weather surveys, activities that are essential for understanding the past climate patterns and predicting future changes.

The significance of studying ice core samples cannot be overstated, as they provide a window into the Earth's climate history, with each layer representing a snapshot of the atmospheric conditions and environmental changes over time. By analyzing these samples, scientists reconstruct past climates and gain valuable insights into the factors that drive global climate variability.

The expedition's objectives were multifaceted, covering a wide range of scientific disciplines. Studies were conducted in meteorology, radio wave propagation, geology, geophysics, oceanography, marine biology, microbiology, upper atmosphere research, chemistry, and glaciology. This comprehensive approach aimed to gain a holistic understanding of the Antarctic environment and its implications for global scientific research. Departing from Goa on 03 December 1983, the expedition spent 95 days in Antarctica, from 26 December to 01 March 1984. Notably, this was the first time an Indian team spent the winter in

Antarctica, thus demonstrating India's commitment to conducting long-term scientific research in the region.

Throughout their stay, the team braved the harsh Antarctic conditions to carry out their scientific work, conducting field studies, collecting data, and collaborating with international researchers. The expedition's success relied on the dedication and expertise of its members, which included Dr Aditi Pant and Prof Sudipta Sengupta, whose contributions helped in advancing our understanding of Antarctica's unique environment and its significance to global scientific research.

One of the key achievements of the expedition was the establishment of *Dakshin Gangotri,* India's first scientific research base station in Antarctica. Located approximately 2,500 km from the South Pole, Dakshin Gangotri was a vital hub for Indian scientific research activities in the region. Aditi Pant's involvement in the expedition extended beyond the initial mission, as she also participated in the fifth expedition to Antarctica in 1984. During this expedition, she continued her research in oceanography and geology, further contributing to India's scientific endeavours in Antarctica. Overall, Aditi Pant's expeditions to Antarctica were instrumental in advancing our understanding of the continent's unique environment and its significance to global scientific research. Her pioneering efforts paved the way for future Indian expeditions to Antarctica and solidified India's position as a key player in international polar research.

Though the team had set out to find out and research much more, living in the harsh conditions of Antarctica was not easy. Life at the Antarctic base camp during the winter was full of challenges and precautions that were necessary for survival in such extreme conditions. It included several lifestyle adaptations like melting ice for water for a routine task, emphasizing the reliance on natural resources, and the need for careful planning to meet basic needs. Even the design of the base camp building was shaped like an E and connected by a corridor for safety and survival. The ability to disconnect the buildings in case of fire underscored the importance of contingency planning and emergency preparedness in remote and isolated environments like Antarctica.

Despite the team's thorough preparation, which included the presence of doctors, helicopters, and ample supplies, they still encountered unexpected challenges. The harsh climate took its toll on perishable items like chillies and onions, which could not withstand the extreme temperatures. As a result, the team had to discard these items, thus leading to a loss of flavour and variety in their meals. There were daily realities of life in Antarctica, where even the most mundane tasks required careful consideration and adaptation to the unforgiving environment. It required the resilience and resourcefulness of those who brave the elements in the pursuit of scientific discoveries and explorations.

Aditi Pant's experience in Antarctica was special and held profound significance for her as an oceanographer. For many in the field, visiting Antarctica represents a dream come true—an opportunity to explore one of the most remote and pristine environments on Earth, and to contribute to the advancement of scientific knowledge. For Aditi, the chance to visit Antarctica was more than just a professional opportunity; it was the realization of a lifelong dream. As an oceanographer, Antarctica held a special allure, an opportunity to study firsthand the unique marine ecosystems, geological features, and climatic conditions of the southernmost continent.

With unwavering determination and enthusiasm, Aditi embraced the chance to explore Antarctica by fully immersing herself in the awe-inspiring beauty and rugged terrain of the continent. Her experience in Antarctica not only fulfilled her professional aspirations but also left an indelible mark on her personal journey as a scientist and adventurer.

Through her work and dedication, Aditi Pant contributed to our collective understanding of Antarctica and its role in shaping global oceanography. Her journey to Antarctica was a testament to the power of dreams, determination, and the pursuit of knowledge in scientific explorations and discoveries.

In 1990, after dedicating 17 years to the NIO, Aditi Pant transitioned to a new chapter in her career by joining the National Chemical Laboratory (NCL) in Pune. At NCL, she shifted her focus to the study of enzymology, particularly exploring the characteristics of salt-tolerant and salt-loving microbes that play crucial roles in the food chain. Aditi Pant's transition to studying the enzymology of salt-tolerant and salt-loving microbes at the NCL marked a significant departure from her previous research focus at the NIO. Despite the shift in research topics and environments, Aditi found the experience in Pune to be equally enriching and educational.

This shift in research emphasis showcased Aditi Pant's versatility as a scientist, as she applied her expertise in microbiology to investigate the biochemical processes underlying the adaptation of microbes to saline environments. By studying the enzymatic activities of these specialized microbes, Aditi Pant aimed to deepen our understanding of their physiological adaptations and ecological significance within the food chain. Her work at the NCL in Pune represented a continuation of her commitment to scientific exploration and discovery. By exploring new avenues of research, she expanded her scientific repertoire and contributed to the advancement of knowledge in the field of microbiology and enzymology. Her transition to NCL marked another significant milestone in her illustrious career, thus demonstrating her ongoing dedication to pushing the boundaries of scientific inquiry.

Aditi Pant's illustrious career was marked by numerous awards, recognitions, and prestigious appointments that underscored her contributions to the field of science and academia. As a Professor Emeritus, Aditi Pant held a distinguished position at the University of Pune, where she made significant contributions to the field of botany through her research, teaching, and mentorship. Aditi Pant's membership in the Maharashtra Society for the Cultivation of Science reflected her active involvement in fostering scientific research and education within the state of Maharashtra. She was also affiliated with the Maharashtra Association for the Cultivation of Science. This further demonstrated her commitment to advancing scientific knowledge and promoting collaborations within the scientific community. Her membership on the Biofuel Committee reflected her expertise in the field of biotechnology and her involvement in initiatives that were aimed at developing sustainable energy solutions. Her fellowship in the Maharashtra Academy of Science is a testament to her exemplary contributions to scientific research and scholarship in Maharashtra.

Aditi Pant's remarkable achievements in the field of science are further exemplified by her ownership of five patents and her extensive publication records, which include over 67 articles in international journals. These patents and publications reflect her innovative contributions to scientific research and her commitment to advancing knowledge in her field. In recognition of her significant contributions to the Indian Antarctic programme, Aditi Pant was honoured with the prestigious Antarctica Award by the Government of India. This award is a testimony to her exceptional dedication, leadership, and achievements in the field of polar research. She shared this honour with esteemed colleagues like Sudipta Sengupta, Jaya Naithani, and Kanwal Vilku, thus highlighting the collaborative nature of scientific explorations and discoveries.

Receiving the Antarctica Award not only acknowledged Aditi Pant's individual accomplishments but also underscored the collective efforts of the entire team in advancing our understanding of Antarctica and its significance toward global scientific research. It is a well-deserved recognition of her outstanding contributions to the Indian Antarctic programme and her lasting impact on polar science.

Throughout her career, Aditi Pant's dedication to scientific inquiry, academic excellence, and service to the scientific community earned her widespread recognition and respect. Her affiliations and appointments underscored her multidisciplinary expertise and her commitment to advancing scientific knowledge and innovation. Her pioneering work in the field of oceanography not only contributed to scientific knowledge but also paved the way for future generations of women scientists in India. As one of the first Indian women to visit Antarctica and make significant contributions to polar research, Aditi Pant shattered gender barriers and inspired countless women to pursue careers in science, particularly in the field of oceanography.

Her decision to join oceanography was driven by the desire to experience freedom. This desire for freedom, both physical and intellectual, guided Aditi's career choices and led her to pursue a path in oceanography. In this field, she found not only an opportunity to travel and explore the world's oceans but also the freedom to engage in scientific inquiry, to question, to innovate, and to contribute to the collective understanding of the natural world. By excelling in a traditionally male-dominated field, Aditi Pant challenged stereotypes and demonstrated that women are equally capable of making valuable contributions to scientific explorations and discoveries. Her achievements serve as a powerful example and encouragement for other women aspiring to pursue careers in oceanography.

8.

Shakuntala Devi

Shakuntala Devi was the first female Mathematician, also known for mental calculations, astrology, and writing, and popularly known as the 'Human Computer'.

Shakuntala Devi was born on 04 November 1929, in Bangalore, Karnataka, India, into a Kannada Brahmin family. Her father, CV Sundararaja Rao, led a fascinating and unconventional life, working in various roles within the entertainment industry. His diverse career included stints as a trapeze artist, lion tamer, tightrope walker, and magician in a circus. His involvement in the circus world exposed Shakuntala Devi to a unique and colourful upbringing, where she witnessed firsthand the spectacle and excitement of circus performances.

Shakuntala Devi's father played a pivotal role in recognizing and nurturing her extraordinary mathematical abilities from a young age. It was during a simple card trick lesson when Shakuntala was around three years old that her father first discovered her remarkable ability to memorize numbers. Impressed by his daughter's innate talent, he decided to harness and showcase Shakuntala's mathematical prowess.

While Shakuntala Devi's father pursued his adventurous career in the circus, she would later become renowned for her extraordinary mathematical talents, a skill that set her apart and earned her international acclaim. Shakuntala Devi's exceptional mathematical abilities continued to develop rapidly during her childhood. By the age of five, she had already mastered solving math problems with remarkable speed and accuracy, thus demonstrating an innate talent for numbers that far surpassed her peers.

In a display of intellect far beyond her years, she effortlessly solved highly complex mental arithmetic problems, leaving onlookers astounded. During her visit to Mysore University, she performed several tricks that demonstrated her strength and unique abilities in the field. It was one of the most monumental events for her that set her on the platform for recognition. As Shakuntala grew, so did her passion for pushing the boundaries of human potential. Driven by a relentless curiosity and a desire to unlock the secrets of the mind, she embarked on a journey of exploration and discovery.

As her mathematical talents became increasingly apparent, Shakuntala Devi began to attract attention and fame. Recognizing his daughter's potential, CV Sundaraja Rao arranged for her to showcase her skills at the circus, where she quickly became a sensation. He decided to leave his career in the circus and embarked on road shows with Shakuntala, where she would demonstrate her incredible ability and perform complex mental calculations with ease. These road shows provided Shakuntala with a platform to showcase her mathematical talent to a wider audience, thereby captivating spectators with her lightning-fast mental arithmetic skills. Under her father's guidance and encouragement, Shakuntala's reputation as a mathematical prodigy began to grow, thus laying the foundation for her future as a celebrated mathematician and performer.

Growing up in a humble household in Bangalore, Shakuntala Devi never had the luxury of formal education. Yet, even in the absence of traditional schooling, her mathematical abilities blossomed with astonishing speed. From counting the petals of flowers in her backyard to solving complex mental arithmetic problems, Shakuntala displayed a natural affinity for mathematics that left those around her in awe.

Despite her focus on mathematics, Shakuntala also had a deep love for literature and writing. In the quiet moments of her childhood, she would often lose herself in the pages of books, immersing herself in stories and poetry. These moments of respite from numbers provided her with a sense of balance and enrichment, thereby nurturing both her analytical and creative faculties.

As Shakuntala's reputation as a mathematician grew, so too did her passion for sharing her knowledge with others. Though her path was unconventional and devoid of formal education, little did she know at that young age that she would go on to become a beacon of inspiration for countless individuals. She would grow to prove that dedication, curiosity, and a love for learning can overcome even the greatest challenges. With *'Mind Dynamics'*, Shakuntala Devi not only cemented her legacy as a mathematical genius but also as a visionary thinker who dared to challenge the boundaries of human perception. Her contributions to the field of mathematics and cognitive science continue to inspire and demonstrate how passion and perseverance can transcend the limitations of circumstances.

With Shakuntala Devi's remarkable talent gaining momentum and recognition, her father recognized the need for a larger stage to showcase her extraordinary abilities. In 1944, he made the bold decision to relocate the family to London, a city brimming with opportunities and a diverse audience that was eager to witness Shakuntala's mathematical prowess. The move to London opened a world of new possibilities for Shakuntala. With its vibrant intellectual and cultural atmosphere, the city provided a fertile ground for her to hone her skills and expand her horizons. From prestigious universities to renowned academic institutions, there was no shortage of platforms for her to dazzle audiences with her remarkable talent.

In London, Shakuntala's unique abilities quickly captured the attention of mathematicians, educators, and the general public. Her demonstrations of lightning-fast mental calculations and feats of mathematical wizardry drew crowds wherever she went, thus solidifying her reputation as a true mathematical prodigy. For Shakuntala, London became more than just a new home; it was a launching pad for her journey to international fame and acclaim. With the support of her family and the newfound opportunities that were afforded by the bustling metropolis, she embarked on a path that would eventually make her a household name around the world. The decision to move to London was a pivotal moment in Shakuntala Devi's life, setting the stage for her meteoric rise to prominence and establishing her as one of the most celebrated mathematical minds of her time.

Shakuntala Devi's journey took her far beyond the borders of her homeland, as she embarked on a whirlwind tour of Europe in 1950. Armed with her extraordinary arithmetic talents, she captivated audiences in countries far and wide, thus leaving a trail of wonder and admiration in her wake. Despite initially facing the challenge of not being fluent in English, Shakuntala's determination and resilience propelled her to overcome linguistic barriers by gradually mastering a variety of languages throughout her travels. Her adventures abroad not only showcased her unparalleled mathematical abilities but also served as a testament to her boundless curiosity and thirst for knowledge. With each new country that she visited, Shakuntala absorbed the culture, language, and customs, thereby enriching her understanding of the world and broadening her horizons in the process.

Shakuntala Devi's tour of Europe was not without its share of memorable moments and remarkable encounters. During one particularly notable appearance on the BBC, she found herself facing off against an interviewer in a battle of mathematical wits. When presented with a challenging calculation, Shakuntala confidently offered her solution, only to be met with scepticism from the interviewer, who believed her answer to be incorrect. However, much to the astonishment of all involved, it was later discovered that Shakuntala's answer was indeed the correct one, thus demonstrating the depth of her mathematical insight and leaving the audience in awe of her exceptional abilities.

A similar incident occurred during Shakuntala's visit to the University of Rome, where she engaged in a spirited exchange with experts and scholars who were eager to put her mathematical prowess to the test. Amidst a flurry of calculations and discussions, Shakuntala confidently provided her answer to a problem, only to be informed by the experts that it was incorrect. Undeterred, Shakuntala stood her ground, prompting the experts to re-examine their own calculations. Much to their surprise, they soon realized that Shakuntala's initial answer had been correct all along, a humbling reminder of the fallibility of even the most seasoned mathematicians and a testament to Shakuntala's unparalleled intuition and precision.

These encounters served as powerful demonstrations of Shakuntala Devi's extraordinary talent and unwavering confidence in her abilities. Whether facing off against interviewers on live television or engaging in scholarly debates at prestigious universities, Shakuntala's brilliance shone through, leaving an indelible impression on all who had the privilege of witnessing her mathematical genius in action.

In the midst of her globetrotting exploits, fate intervened, which led Shakuntala Devi back to her roots in India in the mid-1960s. Here she encountered another significant chapter in her life journey, as she got married to Paritosh Banerji, an esteemed officer of the Indian Administrative Service hailing from Kolkata. In Paritosh, Shakuntala found not only a life partner but also a kindred spirit who shared her passion for exploration and intellectual pursuit. Their union marked the beginning of a new chapter for Shakuntala Devi, one that was filled with love, companionship, and a continued dedication to her lifelong mission of inspiring and empowering others through the beauty of mathematics. Together, Shakuntala and Paritosh embarked on a journey that was marked by love, adventure, and a shared commitment toward making a difference in the world.

Shakuntala Devi's marriage to Paritosh Banerji brought with it both joy and challenges. Despite their deep love and mutual respect for each other, the transition from independence to married life was not without hurdles. Shakuntala, a fiercely independent woman with boundless aspirations and a thirst for exploration, found herself grappling with the constraints of marital expectations and societal norms. As a woman ahead of her time, she struggled with the notion of being 'caged' within the confines of traditional domesticity. Her vibrant spirit and insatiable curiosity yearned for freedom and adventure, yet the responsibilities and expectations of married life threatened to overshadow her aspirations.

Shakuntala Devi's journey as a mother began with the birth of her daughter, Anupama Banerji. For Shakuntala, motherhood was a new chapter that was filled with boundless love, joy, and profound responsibility. Welcoming Anupama into the world brought a newfound sense of purpose and fulfilment to Shakuntala's life, as she embraced the role of nurturing and guiding her daughter with unwavering devotion. As a mother, Shakuntala was determined to instil in Anupama the same sense of independence, curiosity, and resilience that had defined her own life journey. She sought to create a nurturing environment where Anupama could flourish and pursue her own passions and aspirations, while also imparting valuable lessons and wisdom that were gleaned from her own experiences. Shakuntala's deep love for her daughter was evident in every aspect of their relationship, from tender moments shared together to the unwavering support and encouragement which she provided as Anupama navigated the challenges of growing up.

For Shakuntala, marriage was a balancing act between honouring her commitment to her husband and preserving her sense of self and independence. While she cherished her partnership with Paritosh and the love they shared, she also harboured dreams and ambitions that extended beyond the boundaries of their marital union. Navigating these conflicting desires and expectations was a voyage that was fraught with uncertainty and introspection. She grappled with the delicate balance between personal fulfilment and marital harmony, thus seeking solace and guidance in her inner strength and resilience.

The demands of Shakuntala Devi's burgeoning career as a mathematician and performer often took her far from home, thus leaving a significant gap in her personal life and marriage. Constantly travelling for shows and events meant that she spent extended periods away from her husband, Paritosh Banerji, and her daughter, Anupama. The relentless schedule of performances, appearances, and engagements meant that Shakuntala had little time to devote to her personal relationships and domestic life. This constant absence took its toll on her marriage, as the distance and separation strained the bond between Shakuntala and Paritosh.

For Paritosh, watching his wife constantly on the move, travelling from one city to another, was challenging. The physical distance between them led to feelings of loneliness and longing, as he navigated the complexities of married life without Shakuntala by his side. Similarly, Shakuntala's absence had an impact on her relationship with her daughter, Anupama. While she undoubtedly cherished the time they spent together, her frequent travel meant that Shakuntala missed out on many milestones and moments in Anupama's life, since she was unable to be there for her as much as she would have liked.

Despite the challenges posed by Shakuntala's hectic schedule, her family remained a constant source of love and support. Through the ups and downs, they navigated the complexities of balancing career aspirations with personal relationships, while finding strength in their shared bonds and unwavering commitment to each other. The sacrifices made in pursuit of Shakuntala's career took a toll on her personal life and marriage.

In 1976, Shakuntala Devi's visit to New York City captivated audiences with her extraordinary mathematical abilities. Clad in a shimmering blue and green sari, she stood before 80 employees of the State Bank of India at 460 Park Avenue, showcasing her unparalleled talent for mental calculations. With her sari wrapped closely around her, Shakuntala paced back and forth, effortlessly solving a multitude of complex mathematical problems in the blink of an eye. From addition and multiplication to division, she demonstrated her mastery of algorithms —mental shortcuts that even she found challenging to explain.

Despite the presence of Burroughs Model 1700 computers nearby, Shakuntala was not scared and relied solely on her mental prowess to tackle the mathematical queries that were posed to her. With each problem, she provided swift and accurate answers, leaving her audience in awe of her lightning-fast calculations. Shakuntala's capabilities extended beyond 'normal' math problems. She boasted the ability to calculate square and cube roots, as well as logarithms, all within the confines of her mind. Moreover, she possessed an uncanny knack for recalling the days of the week for any given date in the past century, thus showcasing her remarkable memory and mental acuity.

As the queries grew increasingly complex, Shakuntala remained unfazed, confidently delivering correct answers with precision and speed. Whether it was the cube root of 13.824 or the cube root of

188,132,517, Shakuntala's responses were met with astonishment and applause from the audience, thereby confirming her status as a true mathematical prodigy. Her demonstration at the State Bank of India in New York City was yet another testament to Shakuntala Devi's unparalleled talent and the sheer marvel of the human mind. Through her remarkable abilities, she not only inspired admiration but also challenged perceptions of what the human brain is capable of achieving. Through her demonstration, she left an indelible impression on all those present, showcasing the power of the human mind and the beauty of mathematical prowess. As Shakuntala Devi prepared to demonstrate her mathematical prowess at the State Bank of India in New York City, she engaged in conversation with an interviewer, revealing that it was her first visit to the United States. However, when reminded by the interviewer of her previous visit in 1952 to Washington and New York, Shakuntala conceded that her memory had been faulty. This admission of forgetfulness was a rare moment of vulnerability from a woman who was renowned for her exceptional memory and mental abilities.

Despite her remarkable talents, Shakuntala was not immune to the occasional lapse in recollection. Her willingness to acknowledge her mistake with humility only added to her charm and authenticity. Despite the discrepancy in her memory, Shakuntala's performance at the bank was nothing short of extraordinary. With her ability to effortlessly solve complex mathematical problems, she captivated the audience and reaffirmed her status as a mathematical prodigy.

In 1977, Shakuntala Devi also tried her hand at something very different that she had not done before. She got into writing books to share more about her work and experiences. In her book, *Figuring: The Joy of Numbers,* Shakuntala Devi shared insights into the methods she employed to perform mental calculations with remarkable speed and accuracy. Through this book, she aimed to demystify the process of mental arithmetic and empower readers to develop their own mathematical abilities. One of the key techniques that Shakuntala Devi elucidated in *'Figuring'* was the use of mental shortcuts or algorithms to streamline the calculations. These shortcuts allowed her to break down complex mathematical problems into simpler components, thus making them easier to solve mentally. By mastering these algorithms, readers could enhance their computational efficiency and effectively tackle calculations.

Additionally, Shakuntala Devi emphasized the importance of practice and visualization in honing one's mental arithmetic skills. Through repeated practice and visualization of numerical patterns, individuals could sharpen their mental faculties and improve their ability to rapidly and accurately perform calculations. Moreover, the book served as a platform for Shakuntala Devi to share her passion for numbers and instil in readers a sense of wonder and appreciation for the beauty of mathematics. Through engaging anecdotes and examples, she sought to convey the joy and excitement that were inherent in the world of numbers, thus inspiring readers to explore the fascinating realm of mathematics. Overall, *Figuring: The Joy of Numbers* was not just a manual for mental arithmetic but also a celebration of the joy and fascination that numbers can bring. Through her book, Shakuntala Devi left a lasting legacy as a teacher and mentor, guiding readers on a journey of discovery and enlightenment through the enchanting world of mathematics.

She also ventured into the realm of LGBTQ+ studies with her 1977 book, *The World of Homosexuals,* which was a groundbreaking and courageous step. In a time when discussions about homosexuality were often shrouded in silence and stigma, she fearlessly delved into the topic, thus shedding light on the lived experiences of LGBTQ+ individuals in India.

The book, regarded as the first published academic study of homosexuality in India, was met with criticism and controversy.

Shakuntala's decision to explore such a taboo subject matter, particularly in a conservative society, drew scrutiny and backlash from some quarters. However, her motivation stemmed from a deeply personal place—her marriage to a homosexual man. In the documentary *For Straights Only,* she candidly shared her desire to understand homosexuality more deeply, driven by her own experiences and a quest for knowledge and empathy. Her book, *The World of Homosexuals,* was a pioneering work that offered a rare glimpse into the lives of LGBTQ+ individuals in India. Through interviews with homosexual men, discussions with a temple priest, and a review of the existing literature on the subject, Shakuntala sought to paint a comprehensive picture of homosexuality in Indian society. The book culminated in a powerful call for the decriminalization of homosexuality and the need for full acceptance, rather than mere tolerance or sympathy.

Despite its significance, *The World of Homosexuals* largely went unnoticed at the time of its publication. The prevailing social attitudes and taboos surrounding homosexuality may have contributed to its lack of mainstream recognition. However, the book's impact reverberates through history as a pioneering effort to amplify the voices and experiences of the LGBTQ+ individuals in India and advocate for their rights and dignity. Shakuntala Devi's boldness and compassion in addressing this sensitive issue laid the groundwork for future discussions and progress in LGBTQ+ rights in the country.

The marriage between Shakuntala Devi and Paritosh Banerji, once filled with love and mutual respect, began to experience strains and challenges in the years following their union. Various factors contributed to the growing differences between them, including Shakuntala's demanding career and frequent travel, which often took her away from home for extended periods.

However, the most significant turning point in their relationship came during a book promotion event for Shakuntala's groundbreaking work, *The World of Homosexuals*. It was during this event that Shakuntala made the startling claim that her husband, Paritosh, was homosexual. This revelation rocked their marriage to its core and sparked controversy and speculation in both public and private spheres. The revelation of Paritosh's homosexuality, whether true or not, added a new layer of complexity to their already strained relationship. The impact of this revelation, coupled with the challenges they were already facing, ultimately led to their divorce in 1979. The dissolution of their marriage marked the end of an era for Shakuntala and Paritosh, as they parted ways and embarked on separate paths. While the exact details surrounding their divorce remain shrouded in mystery and speculation, the profound impact of their relationship and its subsequent unravelling cannot be understated.

After her divorce, Shakuntala Devi continued to captivate the world with her extraordinary mathematical abilities. On 18 June 1980, she astounded audiences once again with a remarkable demonstration of mental calculations. The Department of Computing at Imperial College London selected two massive 13-digit numbers at random: 7,686,369,774,870 and 2,465,099,745,779. In just 28 seconds, Shakuntala correctly multiplied these numbers, arriving at the staggering answer of 18,947,668,177,995,426,462,773,730. This incredible feat earned Shakuntala Devi a place in the 1982 Guinness Book of World Records, solidifying her status as one of the greatest mathematical prodigies of all time.

Writer Steven Smith aptly remarked that the result was 'so far superior to anything previously reported that it can only be described as unbelievable.' Shakuntala's ability to perform such complex calculations with lightning speed defied conventional understanding and left experts and spectators in awe of her unparalleled talent. Her achievement not only showcased the power of the human mind but also pushed the boundaries of what was thought to be possible in the realm of mathematics.

In 1980, Shakuntala Devi forayed into politics by contesting the Lok Sabha elections as an independent candidate for two constituencies: Mumbai South and Medak in Andhra Pradesh (now in Telangana). In Medak, she stood against the formidable former Prime Minister, Indira Gandhi, declaring her intention to "defend the people of Medak from being fooled by Mrs Gandhi." Despite her spirited campaign efforts, Shakuntala Devi's electoral bid was not successful. In the Medak constituency, she secured the ninth position, garnering 6,514 votes, which accounted for 1.47 per cent of the total votes cast. Though her electoral performance did not yield victory, her decision to enter the political arena underscored her commitment to public service and her desire to advocate for the welfare of the people.

Following her electoral campaign, Shakuntala Devi returned to Bangalore in the early 1980s, where she continued to engage in various pursuits, which included mathematics, writing, and activism. While her political aspirations did not materialize as she had hoped, her bold venture into politics demonstrated her willingness to challenge the status quo and speak out on issues that she deemed important.

In 1988, Shakuntala Devi embarked on a journey to the United States to have her extraordinary abilities studied by Arthur Jensen, a distinguished professor of educational psychology at the University of California, Berkeley. Jensen, known for his research in human intelligence and cognitive abilities, was intrigued by Shakuntala's reputation as a mathematical prodigy and sought to test her skills. During the study, Jensen presented Shakuntala with a series of challenging tasks that included the calculation of large numbers. Among the problems posed to her were the calculation of the cube root of 61,629,875 and the seventh root of 170,859,375. Remarkably, Shakuntala provided the correct solutions to these complex calculations (395 and 15, respectively) in a matter of seconds, astonishing Jensen with the speed and accuracy of her mental arithmetic.

Jensen documented his findings from the study in the academic journal *Intelligence* in 1990, detailing Shakuntala's remarkable performance and the implications of her abilities for our understanding of human intelligence. His research underscored the extraordinary nature of Shakuntala's mathematical talents and provided further validation of her status as one of the greatest mathematical prodigies of all time. Through her collaboration with Arthur Jensen and other researchers, Shakuntala Devi's legacy as a mathematical genius was solidified, leaving an indelible mark in the field of cognitive science and inspiring future generations to explore the mysteries of the human mind.

Shakuntala Devi's talents extended far beyond her extraordinary abilities as a mental calculator. In addition to her prowess in mathematics, she was also a notable astrologer and a prolific author across various genres. Her literary pursuits encompassed a wide range of subjects, thus reflecting her diverse interests and passions. From writing short stories and murder mysteries to penning cookbooks and novels, Shakuntala Devi demonstrated her versatility and creativity as an author. In her works of fiction, she showcased her storytelling prowess, weaving captivating narratives that enthralled readers and kept them on the edge of their seats. Her keen eye for detail and flair for suspense made her murder mysteries particularly engaging, while her cookbooks offered practical insights into the culinary arts, thus reflecting her appreciation for good food and gastronomy.

Beyond her literary endeavours, Shakuntala Devi also had a keen interest in music, which further demonstrated her multifaceted talents and passions. Whether it was through her writings, her mathematical feats, or her explorations in astrology, she left an indelible mark on each field that she ventured into, thereby leaving behind a rich and varied legacy that continues to inspire and captivate audiences around the world.

In her quest to understand the inner workings of the human brain, she developed the groundbreaking concept known as *'Mind Dynamics'*. This was a revolutionary approach to harnessing the power of the mind by utilizing techniques to enhance cognitive abilities and tap into the latent mental faculties. Through her pioneering work, Shakuntala sought to empower individuals to transcend the limitations of their own minds and unlock their untapped potential.

With *'Mind Dynamics'*, Shakuntala Devi not only cemented her legacy as a mathematical genius but also as a visionary thinker who dared to challenge the boundaries of human cognition. Her contributions to the field of mathematics and cognitive science continue to inspire and intrigue researchers and enthusiasts, thus proving that the human mind is capable of extraordinary feats when nurtured and cultivated with passion and dedication.

In April 2013, Shakuntala Devi was admitted to a hospital in Bangalore due to severe respiratory problems. Unfortunately, her health quickly deteriorated over the following two weeks, as she developed complications with her heart and kidneys. Despite the efforts of medical professionals, Shakuntala Devi's condition worsened, and she passed away in the hospital on 21 April 2013.

Her death marked the end of an era for the world of mathematics and beyond. Shakuntala Devi's extraordinary talents, passion for learning, and contributions to various fields left an indelible mark on countless individuals around the globe. Though she may have left this world, her legacy will continue to inspire generations to come, reminding us of the boundless potential of the human mind and the power of perseverance, curiosity, and determination.

9.

Sudha Murthy

Sudha Murthy is an Indian Educator, Author, and Philanthropist. She is the Founder-Chairperson of the non-profit charitable organization Infosys Foundation.

The development of technology companies has been huge during the last two decades in India and worldwide. However, the growth of women in the field of technology has many examples of how women, even though they were better performers, were not given the space and respect to grow in the field as were men. Some women made a path for themselves in ways that carved a future for many women in the field for years to come. One such story is the life of Sudha Murthy, who not only carved a way for herself and her family but also went on to do several things for the betterment of society and the country at large.

Sudha Murthy was born as Sudha Kulkarni into a middle-class family on 19 August 1950. Her father, Dr RH Kulkarni, was a surgeon, and her mother, Vimala Kulkarni, was a school teacher. Sudha's early years were marked by a keen interest in learning and a strong inclination towards academics. Growing up in Shiggaon, Karnataka, Sudha Murthy's environment fostered her academic curiosity and intellectual growth. Encouraged by her parents, she excelled in studies, while showing a particular aptitude for mathematics and science. Her early education was completed in local schools, where she was known for her dedication and brilliant performance.

She was the second child in a family with three daughters and one son. A significant part of her early years was spent with her maternal grandparents. Sudha's maternal grandfather, Sri HR Kadim Diwan, played a crucial role in her formative years. A true Gandhian, he left law school because his teacher suggested that a lawyer might sometimes need to manipulate the truth to win cases. Despite being 63 years older than Sudha, he was her best friend and mentor. He was a scholar who imbued her with a love for books, history, mathematics, and India. His influence instilled in Sudha a free and adventurous spirit, thereby shaping her future pursuits and values.

Her grandmother, although illiterate, was passionate about literature, particularly the works of Triveni, a renowned Kannada writer. Every Wednesday, after finishing her household chores, she would eagerly wait for Sudha to read Triveni's serial *'Kashi Yatre'* to her. One Wednesday, Sudha couldn't keep their reading appointment, which left her grandmother feeling helpless and frustrated. This incident sparked a transformative moment in their relationship. At the age of 12, Sudha took it upon herself to teach her 62-year-old grandmother to read and write. Initially hesitant, her grandmother questioned whether she could learn at her age. Undeterred, Sudha encouraged her and became her teacher. Within a year, her grandmother achieved the remarkable feat of reading the book on her own, demonstrating that age is no barrier to learning. This experience not only strengthened their bond but also highlighted the value of education and empowerment in Sudha's life.

Sudha Murthy's upbringing was marked by a strong emphasis on education and intellectual enrichment. Sudha was raised in an environment that fostered a deep love for learning. Her parents never bought jewellery or expensive clothes for her and her siblings, but they ensured that their home had an extensive library. The Kulkarni household was academically oriented, and education was considered paramount. Her father never purchased a refrigerator, a luxury at the time, but he never hesitated to buy books for his children. This focus on intellectual rather than material wealth profoundly influenced Sudha's values and aspirations in life.

Sudha Murthy's passion for mathematics and science led her to pursue engineering after completing her school education. At a time when engineering was a field that was predominantly occupied by men, Sudha's determination and intellectual prowess shone through. She earned a bachelor's degree in Electrical Engineering from BVB College of Engineering and Technology, thus becoming a trailblazer for women in the field. Her exceptional academic performance was recognized with a gold medal from the then Chief Minister of Karnataka, marking her a standout student. This accolade was a testament to her dedication and resilience in the face of adversity.

Sudha's decision to enter the field of engineering was a bold one that reflected her commitment to breaking gender barriers and challenging societal norms. Her academic journey at BVB College of Engineering and Technology was marked by dedication and excellence. She consistently excelled in her studies by always securing the top position in her class. This achievement was particularly noteworthy given the gender dynamics of the time, thus making her a role model for future generations of female engineers.

In 1968, Sudha Murthy embarked on her journey in engineering by joining the Bachelor of Engineering programme in Electricals at BVB College of Engineering in Hubli. The initial days were challenging and uncomfortable. As the only female student in a college with no provisions for women, such as a ladies' room or a toilet, she had to endure considerable inconveniences. She often waited uncomfortably until she got home to use the bathroom. Recognizing the need, the college authorities eventually built a ladies' toilet on the premises after a year and a half.

Sudha faced significant hurdles beyond just infrastructure. With more than two hundred boys in her class, she was subjected to relentless ragging and teasing. However, her determination to earn her engineering degree was unwavering. No amount of ridicule deterred her from reaching her goal. Her dedication was evident in her perfect attendance record; she did not miss even a single day of class in five years. Sudha understood that if she missed even one day, there would be no one to share the notes with her, thus making her consistent presence crucial to her success.

Over time, the boys who initially teased her began to see her true character and determination. After a year and a half, their attitudes shifted as they realized that she was serious about her education and not just a fleeting presence. Sudha's perseverance and hard work earned her their respect, and many of those who had ragged her became great friends.

Sudha Murthy's academic journey did not end with her bachelor's degree in Electrical Engineering. Encouraged by her father, who was keen that she continue her education, Sudha pursued a Master's degree in Technology (MTech) at the Indian Institute of Science (IISc) in Bangalore, often mistakenly referred to as the Tata Institute of Engineering due to its funding and association with the Tata group. At IISc, Sudha continued to excel in her studies. The rigorous academic environment further honed her technical skills and deepened her understanding of computer science. Her performance was exemplary, and she once again graduated at the top of her class, earning another gold medal for her outstanding achievements. This academic success was not just a personal milestone but also a testament to her dedication and perseverance in a field that was still largely dominated by men.

Sudha Murthy's decision to pursue higher education, particularly in engineering and computer science, was groundbreaking at the time. The societal norms and expectations for women in India during the late

1960s and early 1970s did not include advanced technical education or professional careers. Her accomplishments challenged these norms and paved the way for future generations of women in engineering and technology.

During the last semester of her MTech in Bangalore, Sudha Murthy encountered a notice on the college bulletin board that changed the trajectory of her career. The notice announced that Tata Engineering and Locomotive Co. Ltd (TELCO), now Tata Motors, was seeking young, bright, hardworking engineers through a campus interview. However, the notice ended with a discriminatory line: 'Lady students need not apply.' This blatant exclusion jolted Sudha and spurred her into action. Deeply disturbed by this gender discrimination, Sudha decided to take a bold step.

She purchased a postcard and addressed it to JRD Tata, the Chairman of the Tata Group. In her letter, she expressed her admiration for the philanthropic and innovative legacy of the Tata Group, citing their pioneering efforts in various industries. She then conveyed her disappointment and shame regarding their discriminatory stance towards women students. Sudha wrote: 'Benevolent Tatas who have done so much philanthropic work... innovative Tatas who started the first iron and steel industry, textile industries... I am surprised and ashamed at your attitude toward women students. If you can do this, then anybody can do it'.

A week after sending the postcard, Sudha received a surprising response. She was invited to attend an interview at TELCO's Pune facility, with all expenses covered by the company. Motivated partly by curiosity and partly by the opportunity to visit Pune and purchase saris for friends and relatives, Sudha decided to go for the interview. Sudha was the only person invited for the interview. She attended the interview, armed with determination and a keen sense of justice.

During the interview at TELCO, the interviewing officers presented several reasons for their initial exclusion of female candidates. They explained that the selected engineer would need to work in shifts and drive a jeep, and they also expressed concern that a woman might leave the job after getting married. Sudha Murthy addressed these concerns head-on. She assured the interviewers that she was willing to learn how to drive a jeep and work in shifts, thereby demonstrating her commitment and adaptability. Drawing inspiration from her grandmother, who had learned to read and write at the age of 62 with young Sudha as her teacher, she accepted the challenge of learning to drive at 23. This highlighted her determination and ability to overcome obstacles, just as she had helped her grandmother do so.

Sudha also addressed the assumption that she would quit her job upon marriage. She told the interviewers frankly that while she might leave the company if she got married, she would certainly not leave just because she was a woman. Moreover, she emphasized that she would not quit unless she received a better offer from a rival company. This candid response showcased her professional integrity and commitment to her career, thus breaking down the gender-based assumptions held by the interviewers.

Her boldness and competence impressed the interviewers, and she was offered a position at TELCO, making her the company's first female engineer. Sudha Murthy was taken by surprise when she was offered a job at TELCO in Pune, with a starting salary of Rs 1,500 per month, which was later increased to Rs 5,000 per month. However, the company informed her that they would not provide hostel facilities during her two-year training period on the Shop Floor. Despite these challenges, Sudha felt a moral obligation to accept the position.

At that time, Sudha had plans to continue her education at the prestigious MIT. She was more inclined towards further studies than taking up the job offer from TELCO. However, her father played a crucial role in her decision. He reminded her of the responsibility she bore, particularly after writing so boldly to JRD Tata. Her father chided her for writing the postcard without proper etiquette and emphasized that she couldn't and shouldn't back down now. He explained that rejecting the job offer could potentially harm the chances of other women seeking employment at TELCO in the future. They might use her as a benchmark, and her refusal could set a negative precedent. This sense of responsibility and the potential impact of her actions on future opportunities for women convinced Sudha to take up the job offer.

This milestone was not just a personal achievement but also a significant step forward for gender equality in the engineering sector. Sudha Murthy's appointment at TELCO was a landmark event. It challenged the prevailing norms and opened doors for many other women in the fields of engineering and technology. Her career at TELCO laid the foundation for her future endeavours and set a precedent for inclusivity and diversity in the workplace. This incident was also a turning point for Sudha Murthy. It taught her the importance of insight and the consequences of acting on impulse. She realized the weight of her actions and the broader implications they could have on others. Her decision to join TELCO was driven by a sense of duty and the understanding that her actions could pave the way for other women in this field.

Sudha Murthy joined TELCO Pune in 1974. Her time at TELCO was significant not only for her personal growth but also for the progress it represented for women in the field of engineering. Her presence in the company was a testament to breaking gender barriers and set a precedent for future female engineers.

The Shop Floor had always been a male-dominated domain, and her arrival was met with hostility. The men on the floor were openly rude and resistant, refusing to take orders from a woman and obstructing her efforts to do her job. Tasks were always redirected to a male manager, thus leaving Sudha isolated and frustrated. Despite this unfriendly atmosphere, Sudha's determination remained unwavering. She was clear about her goal: to excel at her work. The hostility hurt, but it did not deter her. She knew she had to overcome these obstacles and was committed to her duties. Instead of wasting energy on minor skirmishes, she decided to save it for the bigger battles ahead.

Initially, she focused on her work with minimal interaction with the men. Sudha realized that a crucial part of overcoming their resistance was effective communication. She understood that half the battle would be won if she could speak the adversary's language. With this in mind, she set about learning the technical and colloquial language that was used by her colleagues. Bridging this gap was essential to gain their respect and cooperation. Gradually, Sudha's dedication and competence began to change the attitudes of those around her. Her technical skills and persistence started speaking for themselves. By focusing on her work and avoiding unnecessary conflicts, she earned the respect of her peers. Over time, the men on the Shop Floor saw her not just as a woman, but as a capable and reliable engineer.

Sudha's time on the Shop Floor turned out to be a significant boon. Her hands-on experience gave her a broader understanding of the mechanical industry than even her husband, Narayana Murthy, the Co-Founder of Infosys. Her work took her to Jamshedpur and Bihar, thus enriching her knowledge and experience. Sudha Murthy's experience at TELCO was a testament to her resilience and strategic thinking. It was a significant chapter in her life that showcased her ability to break through gender barriers and establish herself in a male-dominated field. But her journey did not stop there.

After her groundbreaking tenure at TELCO, Sudha Murty embarked on a new chapter in her career. She joined the Walchand Group of Industries in Pune as a Senior Systems Analyst. This transition marked a significant milestone in Sudha's professional journey, as she brought her wealth of experience and expertise to a new environment. In her new role, Sudha continued to demonstrate her exceptional analytical skills and problem-solving abilities. She delved into the intricacies of systems analysis by working closely with teams to streamline processes and optimize efficiencies. Sudha's keen insights and innovative approaches made her an invaluable asset to the Walchand Group, thereby earning respect and admiration from colleagues and superiors.

Sudha Murty's journey towards love and companionship with Narayana Murthy was a tale woven with the threads of serendipity and humour. Their love story began four years before they exchanged vows in 1978, with an amusing introduction that left Sudha puzzled and intrigued. It all started with Sudha's friend, Prasanna, who would bring her a book every day with Narayana Murthy's name inscribed on the first page alongside various exotic locations. *'Narayana Murthy Istanbul'*, *'Narayana Murthy Peshawar'*, the unusual dedication sparked Sudha's curiosity. She couldn't help but wonder if this mysterious Narayana Murthy was some sort of international bus conductor, traversing the globe with his name scribbled in books. With such whimsical notions in mind, Sudha's expectations were quite different from when she finally laid eyes on Narayana Murthy for the first time.

Reality painted a different picture. Despite the initial discrepancy between her imagination and reality, Sudha found herself drawn to Narayana's charm and intellect. As they spent more time together, they formed a deep connection which blossomed into friendship, which soon blossomed into love. Their shared interests, mutual respect, and genuine affection laid the foundation for a relationship that would stand the test of time.

Contrary to Sudha's initial expectations, Narayana Murthy turned out to be quite different from the image she had conjured in her mind. Shy, bespectacled, and introverted, he was far from the adventurous international traveller that she had imagined. Nevertheless, Sudha found herself drawn to his quiet demeanour and intellectual depth. When Narayana extended an invitation for dinner, Sudha was initially taken aback. She hesitated, feeling apprehensive about the suddenness of the invitation, especially since she was the only girl in the group. However, Narayana's persistence and the camaraderie of their friends eventually convinced her to accept. The group agreed to meet for dinner the next day at 7:30 pm at the Green Fields hotel on the main road in Pune.

As Sudha and Narayana spent more time together, their conversations delved into Narayana's experiences abroad and the books that had left a lasting impact on him. Sudha found herself captivated by Narayana's insights and perspectives, and enjoyed their intellectually stimulating exchanges. Meanwhile, Sudha's friends couldn't help but notice Narayana's efforts to impress her with his stories and knowledge. They speculated that his interest in Sudha ran deeper than mere friendship. Despite their suggestions, Sudha remained sceptical, dismissing the idea that Narayana had romantic intentions.

However, one evening, after a particularly engaging dinner, Narayana broached a topic that Sudha had been both anticipating and dreading. He confessed to Sudha with utmost sincerity, revealing his insecurities and limitations. "I am 5'4" tall. I come from a lower-middle-class family. I can never become rich in my life, and I can never give you any riches," he confessed. Moved by his candid honesty and vulnerability, Sudha was momentarily taken aback. She listened intently as Narayana continued, acknowledging Sudha's beauty, intelligence, and potential to choose anyone she desired. "But will you marry me?" he asked, his earnest gaze searching for her response. Caught off guard by Narayana's heartfelt proposal, Sudha asked for some time to consider his question.

Sudha's decision to share Narayana's proposal with her parents sparked a flurry of mixed reactions within her family. While her mother expressed optimism and approval, recognizing Narayana's intelligence and familial background, her father remained sceptical and apprehensive.

Concerned about Sudha's future and well-being, her father voiced his reservations about Narayana's suitability as a life partner. He harboured doubts about Narayana's career prospects, financial stability, and aspirations, particularly his desire to pursue a career in politics and establish an orphanage. When the time came for Narayana to meet Sudha's parents in Pune, his initial absence and subsequent arrival in a flamboyant red shirt only served to exacerbate her father's concerns.

Despite Narayana's explanation of a work-related delay and his sincere efforts to make amends, Sudha's father remained unimpressed. Narayana's candid admission of his ambitions to join the communist party and establish an orphanage further solidified her father's apprehensions. He questioned Narayana's ability to support a family and provide stability, thus ultimately delivering a resolute verdict: he did not approve of Sudha marrying someone with such uncertain prospects.

Sudha found herself caught between her own desires and her father's reservations, torn between her love for Narayana and her familial obligations. It was a difficult moment, one that would test Sudha's resolve and resilience as she navigated the complexities of love, family, and personal aspirations. Caught in the midst of conflicting desires and loyalties, Sudha found herself in a precarious situation. While she was deeply committed to Narayana and could not imagine marrying anyone else, she also cherished her father's wishes and sought his approval for their union.

Despite her father's insistence that Narayana take up a steady job, he remained resolute in his principles. He refused to compromise his values or ambitions for the sake of meeting someone else's expectations, even if it meant risking his relationship with Sudha. For three long years, Sudha grappled with this impasse, torn between her love for Narayana and her desire to honour her father's wishes. Their courtship took them to every restaurant and cinema hall in Pune, yet the underlying tension remained unresolved. Throughout this period, Sudha remained steadfast in her commitment to both Narayana and her father.

As the deadlock persisted in Sudha and Narayana's courtship, Narayana made a significant career move. He took a bold step and quit his job as a research assistant to start his own software business. Sudha found herself shouldering the responsibility of supporting Narayana financially, even as she navigated the complexities of their relationship. During the late 1970s, as computers began to make a significant impact in India, Narayana decided to pursue a job opportunity as General Manager at Patni Computers in Bombay. However, before he could join the company and embark on training in the US, he expressed his desire to marry Sudha. Seeing Narayana's newfound stability and promising career prospects, Sudha's father finally relented, giving his blessings to their union.

On 10 February 1978, Sudha and Narayana were married in Narayana's house in Bangalore, with only their two families present to witness the joyous occasion. It was a modest affair, which reflected the simplicity and humility of the couple. Sudha adorned her first silk sari, a cherished symbol of their union. Despite their limited financial resources, the wedding expenses amounted to only Rs 800 (approximately US $17), with Sudha and Narayana each contributing Rs 400. Their wedding was a testament to their love, determination, and resilience. Despite the challenges they faced along the way, Sudha and Narayana's bond grew stronger with time. Together, they embarked on a journey that was filled with shared dreams, mutual respect, and unwavering support for each other's aspirations.

After their wedding, Sudha embarked on a new adventure with Narayana by her side. They travelled together to the United States, where Narayana had to start training for his new job. Narayana, ever supportive of Sudha's passions and knowing her love for travel and adventure, encouraged her to explore America on her own. Eager to seize the opportunity, Sudha set off on a solo backpacking journey across America. For three months, she immersed herself in the sights, sounds, and experiences of this vast and diverse country. From bustling cities to serene landscapes, Sudha ventured far and wide, embracing each new encounter with enthusiasm and curiosity. Her journey was filled with memorable experiences and encounters, from meeting fellow travellers or being taken into custody by the New York police because they thought she was an Italian who was trafficking drugs in Harlem, to spending the night at the bottom of the Grand Canyon with an old couple.

In 1981, Narayana Murthy harboured a bold vision to start Infosys, a venture that would revolutionize the Indian software industry. Despite his lack of capital, he possessed an unwavering determination to turn his dream into reality. Initially, Sudha harboured reservations about Narayana venturing into the business world. With no background in entrepreneurship and a comfortable life in Bombay, Sudha was reluctant to take the risk of starting a new venture.

Despite her apprehensions, Sudha recognized Narayana's passion and commitment toward creating high-quality software. She made a momentous decision to support him wholeheartedly, thus demonstrating her unwavering faith in his abilities. In a remarkable display of trust and solidarity, Sudha contributed her secret savings of Rs 10,000, which were earmarked for a rainy day, to Narayana's endeavour. With this financial backing, Sudha effectively provided Narayana with a three-year sabbatical, thereby relieving him of any immediate financial worries as he pursued his entrepreneurial dreams. She assured him that she would manage the household finances during this period, thus allowing him to focus entirely on building Infosys.

As Infosys grew and became a big tech giant in India, Sudha stepped back to take care of her children and family. She had understood from Narayana that either of them would be involved in a role at Infosys and not both. She understood the reason that in the growing phase 100 per cent had to be given, and it would not be fair to their children and family. Narayana was also supportive and willing to step back and let Sudha take a more active role if she desired, but Sudha understood that Infosys was his dream, so she was content to have a balanced family and life, as she knew her husband trusted and was confident about her abilities and skills. She had nothing to prove. Yet she continued to do different things in life.

Sudha Murthy's dedication to education and her commitment to imparting knowledge extended beyond her technical expertise. Despite her numerous responsibilities and achievements, Sudha found fulfilment in teaching computer science to MBA and MCA students at Christ University. Teaching provided Sudha with not only a source of income, but also a sense of personal satisfaction and fulfilment. Despite her financial independence, Sudha valued the opportunity to contribute to the academic growth and development of students. Her role as a teacher allowed her to share her wealth of knowledge and experience with the next generation, thus inspiring them to pursue excellence in their chosen fields. Even though teaching was not a necessity for Sudha, she embraced it as a means of giving back to society and making a meaningful impact in the lives of others. Through her role as an educator, Sudha continued to embody the values of lifelong learning, humility, and service to others.

Sudha Murthy is also an acclaimed author with a prolific body of work that includes novels, travelogues, collections of short stories, and children's books. Her writing reflects her deep empathy and understanding of human nature and societal issues. Some of her notable works include *Wise and Otherwise, Dollar Bahu, Three Thousand Stitches,* and *The Day I Stopped Drinking Milk*. Her books have been translated into multiple languages and are cherished by readers of all ages.

Sudha Murthy established Infosys Foundation in 1997 with a single mission: to uplift and empower the underprivileged segments of society. Over the past three decades, her endeavours have encompassed a diverse range of initiatives that are aimed at fostering positive change in communities across India. Her efforts have led to the establishment of hospitals, orphanages, rehabilitation centres, school buildings, science centres, and more than 3,500 libraries. These endeavours have touched the lives of countless individuals, particularly in rural areas, where her focus is on supporting women and children.

As one of the trustees of the Infosys Foundation, Sudha is deeply involved in philanthropic endeavours, traversing approximately 800 villages across six states: Karnataka, Tamil Nadu, Andhra Pradesh, Odisha, Chandigarh, and Maharashtra. Despite her minimal staff, which comprises trustees and office members, Sudha remains committed to her goals with unwavering dedication and diligence. The distinct identity of the Infosys Foundation is a testament to Sudha's tireless efforts and collective resolve. Through her relentless pursuit of social impact and community development, she strives to create a more equitable and inclusive society, where every individual has the opportunity to thrive and realize their full potential.

Sudha Murthy went on to receive many awards and honours in life. Her literary contributions have been recognized with numerous awards, which include the RK Narayan Award for Literature, the Padma

Shri in 2006 for her contribution to social work, and several honorary doctorates. Sudha is known to be a very happy and content person in life who faces challenges head-on. Her family deeply values having her by their side so that they can do bigger things in life.

Though Sudha knows that she had to make certain choices in life, it does not mean that she lost herself in the journey. She has been thoroughly supported by everyone and knows that she has become a source of inspiration for many. Not only is she a true leader as a woman in the field of technology, but her attitude toward life and nature, in spite of achieving so much in life is also commendable and a source of motivation for men and women across India.

10.

Tessy Thompson

Tessy Thomas is an Indian Aerospace Engineer and former Director-General of Aeronautical Systems, and the former Project Director for Agni-IV Ballistic Missile in the Defence Research and Development Organization (DRDO).

Over the last few years, some science fields have seen a high commitment and interest from women scientists in India. It is not like there weren't enough women earlier to be able to take on such deeply technical and analytical roles, but it is more like they were not given the space and time to think about how and what they could contribute to this field.

Dr Tessy Thomas, born in April 1963, comes from a Syro-Malabar Catholic family in Alappuzha, Kerala, India. Her name, Tessy, is derived from Teresa or Tressia, in honour of Mother Teresa, thus reflecting a tradition of naming children after revered figures. Dr Tessy Thomas received her early education from St Michael's Higher Secondary School and St Joseph's Girls' Higher Secondary School in her hometown, Alappuzha, Kerala. From an early age, Dr Tessy Thomas demonstrated a natural flair for mathematics and physics.

During her pre-degree years in college, she excelled academically, scoring a perfect hundred per cent in mathematics. Her proficiency in mathematics was complemented by her outstanding performance in science, where she scored more than 95 per cent. These exceptional academic achievements highlighted her strong analytical and problem-solving skills, thereby laying a robust foundation for her future studies and career. Her remarkable aptitude in these subjects not only underscored her intellectual capabilities but also fuelled her passion for pursuing a technical career.

Dr Tessy Thomas spent her childhood near the Thumba Rocket Station in Kerala, which is one of India's primary space launch stations. Growing up in such a vicinity played a significant role in shaping her interests and aspirations. During her school days, the world was abuzz with the news of NASA's Apollo missions, particularly as the Apollo vehicle was about to land on the moon. This historic event captured the imagination of people around the globe, including young Tessy.

Hearing about the Apollo missions daily sparked a sense of wonder and inspiration in her. The idea that humans could build a vehicle that was capable of reaching the moon and beyond fascinated her. This inspiration planted a seed in her mind that one day she, too, could be part of creating rockets that could touch the sky. Her proximity to the Thumba Rocket Station and the excitement which surrounded space exploration fuelled her passion for rockets and missiles. This early fascination grew into a strong interest in missile technology, which she pursued with determination.

Dr Tessy Thomas grew up in a supportive and education-oriented family, with four sisters and one brother. Her parents placed a high value on education, thus ensuring that all six siblings received proper schooling and encouraged each child to pursue careers that were aligned with their own interests and strengths. This nurturing environment fostered a sense of ambition and determination among the children, thereby allowing them to excel in their chosen fields. The emphasis on education and personal development was a cornerstone of the Thomas family's values. This supportive background played a crucial role in Tessy Thomas's journey towards becoming a prominent figure in India's missile technology sector.

At the age of 13, her family faced a significant challenge when her father suffered a stroke that left the right side of his body paralyzed. In response to this life-altering event, her mother, who was a teacher, decided to become a housewife to take care of the family and manage the household. Despite these difficulties, Tessy Thomas continued to excel academically and showed remarkable resilience. Her early experiences instilled in her a strong sense of determination and perseverance, the traits that became crucial for her future career.

Her parents' dedication to providing quality education and their encouragement to follow individual passions contributed to her and her siblings' successes. Dr Tessy Thomas's interest in solid-state physics was nurtured by her mother, who played a pivotal role in encouraging her academic pursuits. Recognizing Tessy's enthusiasm for science, her mother supported and guided her, thus fostering an environment that valued education and intellectual curiosity. This encouragement was crucial in shaping Tessy's aspirations and provided her with the confidence to pursue a career in a field that fascinated her.

To formalize her aspirations and gain a solid foundation in the technical aspects of her interests, Dr Thomas pursued a degree in engineering. She graduated from the Government Engineering College, Thrissur, with a focus on engineering, which equipped her with the necessary skills and knowledge.

Dr Tessy Thomas's journey to becoming a prominent scientist was marked by both academic excellence and personal determination. To pursue her engineering studies at the Government Engineering College, Thrissur, she took an education loan of ₹100 per month from the State Bank of India. This financial assistance was crucial in enabling her to afford her education and live in a hostel, thus providing her with the environment that was needed to focus on her studies.

In addition to the loan, Dr Thomas's outstanding academic performance earned her a scholarship that covered her tuition fees. Her entry into the first 10 students of the merit list during her admissions secured this scholarship, which highlighted her exceptional abilities and dedication to her studies. This financial support not only eased the burden on her family but also motivated her to continue excelling academically. Living in a hostel during her BTech allowed Dr Thomas to immerse herself fully in her educational pursuits, while being surrounded by peers and resources that further enhanced her learning experience.

The combination of an education loan and scholarship provided her with the courage and means to pursue her engineering degree without being hindered by financial constraints. Her academic journey did not stop there; she further specialized by earning an MTech in Guided Missiles from the Institute of Armament Technology, Pune (now known as the Defence Institute of Advanced Technology). This specialization allowed her to delve deeper into the intricacies of missile technology and solid-state physics, which helped her align her academic background with her career goals. She was selected among the top 10 students for the DRDO-sponsored MTech programme in Guided Missiles. This prestigious selection highlighted her academic prowess and potential in the field of defence technology.

At the age of twenty, Tessy Thomas embarked on a journey that shaped her future and the future of India's defence capabilities. She enrolled in the Institute of Armament Technology (now the Defence Institute of Advanced Technology) to pursue the career of her dreams. Little did she know what the future held for her. This decision marked the beginning of an extraordinary career in missile science, which was driven by her passion for engineering and her desire to contribute to her country's security. As Tessy walked the halls of the institute, she felt a mix of excitement and determination. The rigorous curriculum challenged her, but she thrived on the intensive study and hands-on experience that the programme offered. Each lecture and laboratory session brought her closer to understanding the complexities of missile technology. Her professors recognized her exceptional talent and dedication, thus predicting a bright future for the young scientist.

It was during this transformative period that Tessy met Saroj Kumar Patel, a fellow student at the institute. Saroj was focused and driven, sharing Tessy's passion for science and technology. The two quickly became friends, bonding over long study sessions and their mutual aspirations. Their friendship blossomed into romance, which was marked by late-night discussions about their dreams and the future of India's defence.

Saroj's ambition was no less formidable than Tessy's. He aspired to serve his country with distinction in the Indian Navy. As their relationship deepened, they realized that their shared commitment to their careers would be a cornerstone of their partnership. They encouraged and supported each other, thereby finding strength in their common goals. Tessy and Saroj continued to support each other's careers. Saroj rose through the ranks of the Indian Navy, eventually becoming a commodore. Their partnership, built on mutual respect and shared goals, was a source of strength and inspiration for both. They soon decided to get married and had a son. Very fondly, Tessy named him 'Tejas'. He shared his name with India's first homegrown Light Combat Aircraft (also developed by DRDO). Actually, it is an anagram of his mother's and father's names.

Dr Tessy Thomas's early academic successes in mathematics and science foreshadowed her future accomplishments. Despite facing significant familial challenges, which included her father's debilitating stroke when she was very young, she remained steadfast in her pursuit of education and her career goals. Her father's health and her mother's decision to transition were a big change in her family. But none of this got in the way of Dr Thomas as she had big dreams of studying hard and pursuing her dream to do something big. This period of hardship could have derailed her ambitions, but instead, it strengthened her resolve.

The support and encouragement from her family played a crucial role in her perseverance. Her parents, committed to ensuring that all their children receive a proper education, fostered an environment where academic excellence and personal aspirations were highly valued. This supportive backdrop was instrumental in helping Dr Thomas overcome the obstacles that were posed by her family's circumstances. Her natural aptitude for mathematics and science, combined with her unwavering determination, propelled her through her educational journey. She excelled during her pre-degree years, thus achieving perfect scores in mathematics and near-perfect scores in science, which laid a strong foundation for her future studies.

Upon completing her master's degree in 1986, Dr Thomas began her career as a faculty member at the Institute of Armament Technology (IAT), Pune, specializing in Guided Missiles. Her role as an educator allowed her to contribute to the development of future defence scientists and engineers while deepening her own expertise in missile technology.

After two years at IAT, she joined the Defence Research and Development Laboratory (DRDL) in Hyderabad. It was at DRDL that she had the opportunity to work under the guidance of Dr APJ Abdul Kalam, who was the director of the laboratory at that time. Dr Kalam, a renowned Aerospace Scientist and later the President of India, had a profound influence on her. His vision, dedication, and innovative approach to missile technology inspired her in many ways. Under Dr Kalam's mentorship, Dr Tessy Thomas honed her skills and contributed to several critical missile development projects.

Her initial work focused on the design and development of the guidance system for the Agni missile, a crucial component of India's strategic defence arsenal. Recognizing her exceptional skills and potential, Dr Kalam invited her to join a specialized team of 50 scientists who were working on the inertial navigation systems for the Agni-guided missiles. Dr Kalam, who was known for his visionary approach to missile technology, played a significant role in shaping Dr Thomas's career. He had a unique perspective on missiles, famously stating, "Missiles are not weapons of destruction; missiles are weapons of peace. Strength respects strength." This philosophy emphasized the role of missiles in maintaining peace through strength and deterrence, rather than mere destruction.

Under Dr Kalam's mentorship, Dr Thomas wholeheartedly embraced this vision. She was inspired by his dedication and the sense of mission that he instilled in the team. Dr Kalam's belief in the power of scientific and technological strength to secure peace deeply influenced her. She took his vision to heart and committed herself to advancing the Agni missile programme, since she understood its critical role in ensuring national security and fostering a balance of power.

Dr Thomas contributed significantly to the Agni missile programme. She worked diligently on developing the guidance and navigation systems that are vital for the missile's precision and reliability. Her expertise and leadership have been instrumental in the success of the various phases of the Agni project, which has become a cornerstone of India's strategic defence capabilities. Dr Tessy Thomas's association with the Agni missile programme began with its developmental flights, thereby marking the start of a dedicated and impactful career in missile technology. She devoted countless hours toward studying and researching various aspects of the project, hence demonstrating an exceptional work ethic and a deep commitment to advancing India's defence capabilities.

A pivotal moment in her career came when she was tasked with designing the guidance scheme for Long-Range Missile Systems, which would be utilized in the Agni missile. This challenge was significant due to the complex requirements of the missile's flight trajectory. The Agni missiles had to travel beyond the Earth's atmosphere and then reenter at extremely high speeds, by generating temperatures exceeding 3,000 degrees Celsius. Dr Thomas led a team of scientists in developing an innovative energy management guidance scheme, a critical technology for long-range missiles. This scheme had to ensure precise control over the missile's trajectory, manage the immense energy generated during reentry, and ensure that the missile could withstand the extreme thermal conditions which it would encounter.

Her leadership and technical expertise were crucial in overcoming these challenges. The successful development of this guidance scheme was a first for India, thereby marking a significant milestone in the country's missile technology capabilities. It not only enhanced the performance and reliability of the Agni missiles but also positioned India as a formidable player in the field of strategic defence.

Dr Tessy Thomas served as the Associate Project Director of the 3,000 km range Agni-III missile project, thus playing a crucial role in its development and success. Her expertise and leadership were pivotal in the successful firing of the Agni-III missile, which has a range of 3,500 km. The Agni-III missile project was a significant advancement in India's strategic missile programme, which was capable of carrying nuclear warheads and enhancing India's deterrence capabilities.

Dr Thomas's contributions to the project included overseeing the development of critical technologies, ensuring the precision and reliability of the missile's guidance and navigation systems, and managing the complex logistics and coordination which were required for successful test launches. Her work on the Agni-III missile was instrumental in achieving key milestones for the project, thus demonstrating her ability to lead high-stakes, technologically advanced projects. The successful firing of the Agni-III missile was a testament to her technical acumen, project management skills, and dedication to India's defence technology.

During the years following the Agni-II and Agni-III tests and launches, Tessy Thomas navigated the challenging balance between her roles as a dedicated defence scientist and a homemaker. Her unwavering commitment to her work demanded significant sacrifices, thereby pushing her to prioritize her duties as a scientist even when personal challenges arose. As a mother, Tessy was deeply devoted to her family. She cherished her time with her son, Tejas, and worked hard to ensure that he was well cared for. However, her role in the development and testing of India's strategic missile programme required immense dedication and focus. There were moments when her professional responsibilities took precedence, thus forcing her to make tough decisions.

One such instance occurred when Tejas fell ill. Despite her deep concern for her son, Tessy's commitment to the Agni missile programme required her presence at a critical missile launch. She made the difficult decision of leaving Tejas in the care of family members and colleagues, trusting that they would provide the necessary support and care in her absence. This sacrifice underscored the intensity and demands of her work, as well as her belief in the importance of her contributions to national defence. Balancing her dual roles was not easy, and Tessy often walked a tightrope between her personal and professional lives. Her ability to manage these competing demands showcased her extraordinary resilience and determination. She found ways to excel in her career while ensuring that her family received the love and attention that they needed.

Following the successful testing of the Agni-III missile, Dr Tessy Thomas was appointed the Project Director for the Agni-IV missile project. This role involved leading the development of a state-of-the-art missile system that incorporated many new technologies for the first time. Under her leadership, the Agni-IV missile was successfully flight-tested and proven. Dr Thomas faced significant challenges during this project, especially after the initial test of the Agni-II Prime (later designated as Agni-IV) failed. Despite this setback, she was tasked with identifying the reasons for the failure and implementing corrective measures. Her dedication and technical expertise were crucial in addressing these issues and ensuring the success of subsequent tests.

"The missile's first test was a failure. But not a total failure, as the first stage of the missile went off well. Finally, we had an excellent launch," Dr Thomas said, thereby highlighting the partial successes and learning from the initial test to achieve a flawless final launch. In 2012, the Agni-IV missile was successfully tested, thus marking a significant milestone for India's strategic missile capabilities. Agni-IV, India's longest-range nuclear-capable missile at that time, could hit targets up to 3,500 kilometres away. This achievement demonstrated not only the technical advancements in missile technology but also Dr Thomas's effective leadership and problem-solving skills.

Dr Tessy Thomas's achievements with the Agni-IV project solidified her reputation as a leading scientist in missile technology. Her role in overcoming technical challenges and ensuring the project's success showcases her exceptional leadership and technical expertise. Her work not only advanced India's defence capabilities but also inspired many young scientists, particularly women, to pursue careers in science and technology.

In 2009, Tessy Thomas reached a new pinnacle in her illustrious career when she was appointed the Project Director of the Agni-V missile project. This ambitious project aimed to develop a missile with an impressive range of 5,000 kilometres, further bolstering India's strategic defence capabilities. As Project Director, Tessy faced immense pressure with high expectations. The Agni-V missile was designed to be a game-changer in India's missile arsenal, which was capable of delivering a nuclear payload over long distances with great precision. This required advanced technology and meticulous planning, from the design phase through to the final testing.

Under her leadership, the project saw significant advancements. Tessy and her team worked tirelessly, overcoming numerous technical and logistical challenges. Their dedication and hard work paid off when the Agni-V missile was successfully tested on 19 April 2012. This successful launch marked a significant milestone for India's defence programme, thus showcasing the country's capability to develop and deploy long-range missiles. The successful testing of Agni-V was a moment of immense pride for Tessy and her team. It demonstrated not only their technical prowess but also their ability to innovate and execute complex projects. The achievement was celebrated across the nation and recognized internationally, thereby establishing India as a significant player in the field of missile technology.

Dr Tessy Thomas reflected on the successful test of the Agni-V missile as "an indescribable and great" moment in her career. She vividly recalled the tension and excitement as the missile embarked on its flight path. "We watched breathlessly, praying for inner strength as the missile took off on its flight path," she recounts. The pressure was immense as they monitored the missile's trajectory, but the flight prediction chart provided reassuring updates. When the missile finally reached its intended destination, a wave of relief and triumph swept over the team.

"We said to each other, 'We have done it,'" Tessy recalls, while capturing the collective pride and accomplishment of her team.

After the launch, Tessy felt a strong urge to share the success with her former boss and mentor, Dr APJ Abdul Kalam. She visited him, eager to convey the news and seek his blessings. Dr Kalam, a revered figure in Indian science and a source of inspiration for countless scientists, received her warmly. "He is a role model for all our Indian scientists," Tessy said, with her voice filled with emotion. Dr Kalam praised the team's hard work and dedication by acknowledging the significant achievement. As a token of his appreciation, he gifted Tessy his latest book of poems. This gesture, coming from someone she deeply admired, was profoundly moving for her.

The journey to this moment had been filled with challenges and sacrifices. Balancing her roles as a defence scientist and a homemaker, Tessy often found herself making difficult choices, such as leaving her unwell son, Tejas, to ensure her presence at critical missile launches. Yet, her perseverance and dedication to her work never wavered. The success of the Agni-V missile was a testament to her commitment, expertise, and the unwavering support of her team and family.

Dr Tessy Thomas fondly remembers the time when Dr Kalam walked through the corridors of the DRDO, stopping by each desk to leave a word of encouragement. For the juniors, having the director personally acknowledge their work was a significant morale booster. "It was a big thing for juniors at that time to have a director acknowledge us," Tessy recalls. This practice wasn't just about recognition; it was about building a culture of support and encouragement, a culture that Dr Kalam left behind for others to follow.

Tessy always found inspiration from Dr Kalam, not just for his scientific achievements but for his leadership and the way he valued every team member's contribution. His habit of offering personal words of encouragement instilled a sense of belonging and motivation among the staff. Dr Kalam's belief in fostering a nurturing and appreciative work environment impacted Tessy and many of her colleagues profoundly.

His approach was not merely about scientific progress but about human connection and empowerment. Dr Kalam's ability to see potential in everyone and his efforts to inspire them to achieve greatness left a lasting legacy at DRDO. Tessy internalized these lessons, thus carrying forward this culture of encouragement and support in her own leadership roles. As she progressed in her career, Tessy embodied the values that Dr Kalam had instilled. She made it a point to acknowledge and encourage her team, understanding the powerful impact that such gestures had on their motivation and performance. Tessy's leadership style, shaped by Dr Kalam's influence, helped in fostering a collaborative and innovative environment within her teams.

Dr Kalam's influence on Tessy extended beyond professional guidance. He was a role model whose principles and actions provided her with a blueprint for effective leadership and compassionate mentorship. Tessy's journey from a young scientist to the Project Director of major missile projects was significantly shaped by the inspiration and lessons that she drew from Dr Kalam. Even Dr Kalam would quote Dr Tessy Thomas as a woman of inspiration and tell all youngsters about her.

In addition to her remarkable contributions to India's missile programmes, Dr Tessy Thomas pursued further academic excellence to enhance her knowledge and skills. In 2014, she earned a PhD in Missile Guidance from Jawaharlal Nehru Technological University (JNTU), Hyderabad. This advanced degree reflected her deep commitment to the field of missile technology and her desire to contribute to its advancement through rigorous research and innovation. Balancing her demanding career and academic pursuits, Dr Thomas also obtained an MBA in Operations Management from Indira Gandhi National Open

University (IGNOU) in 2007. This degree equipped her with essential management skills, hence enabling her to effectively lead complex projects and teams within the DRDO. Her PhD in Missile Guidance provided her with a deep understanding of the intricacies of missile technology, while her MBA in Operations Management helped her in streamlining operations and improving efficiencies within her teams.

On 01 June 2018, Dr Tessy Thomas assumed the role of Director-General, Aeronautical Systems, at the DRDO, marking yet another significant milestone in her distinguished career. In this prestigious position, she oversaw aeronautical research and development initiatives while playing a pivotal role in advancing India's capabilities in aerospace technology. During her tenure as Director-General, Dr Thomas brought her extensive experience and expertise to a wide range of aeronautical projects. Her leadership was instrumental in driving innovation and progress in areas such as aircraft designs, propulsion systems, avionics, and Unmanned Aerial Vehicles (UAVs). Under her guidance, DRDO made significant strides in developing cutting-edge technologies to bolster India's defence capabilities in the aerospace domain.

Throughout her tenure, Dr Thomas remained committed toward fostering a culture of excellence and collaboration within the DRDO's aeronautical systems division. She encouraged interdisciplinary cooperation and knowledge-sharing, thus leveraging the diverse talents of the organization's scientists and engineers to tackle complex challenges and achieve breakthroughs in aerospace technology.

Dr Tessy Thomas's tenure as Director-General also saw renewed focus on research and development partnerships with academia, industry, and international collaborators. These collaborations facilitated the exchange of ideas, resources, and expertise, thereby accelerating progress and enhancing India's position as a global leader in aerospace innovation. During her 32-year tenure with the Agni missile programme, Dr Thomas made significant contributions across various domains, which included guidance, control, inertial navigation, trajectory simulation, and mission design. Her expertise and leadership played a pivotal role in the successful development and testing of multiple Agni missile variants, with each contributing to India's strategic deterrence capabilities.

Dr Tessy Thomas's illustrious career has been punctuated by numerous accolades and honours, which recognize her exceptional contributions to the field of missile technology and her exemplary leadership in the scientific community. As a testament to her expertise and accomplishments, Dr Thomas has been elected as a Fellow at esteemed institutions such as the Indian National Academy of Engineering (INAE), the Institution of Engineers-India (IEI), and the Tata Administrative Service (TAS). These recognitions underscore her standing as a distinguished figure in the field of engineering and technology.

Among her notable awards, Dr Thomas was honoured with the Lal Bahadur Shastri National Award for her pivotal role in making India self-reliant in the realm of missile technology. This prestigious award reflects her significant contributions to India's defence capabilities and her dedication to advancing indigenous defence research and development. In 2018, Dr Thomas was bestowed with the Dr Thomas Cangan Leadership Award at the Faculty of Management Studies – Institute of Rural Management, Jaipur (FMS-IRM). This recognition highlights her exceptional leadership qualities and her ability to inspire and empower others in the pursuit of excellence.

Further adding to her impressive list of accolades, Dr Thomas was honoured with the Lokmanya Tilak National Award in 2022, which recognized her outstanding contributions to science and technology, and her exemplary service to the nation. In 2023, Dr Thomas was recognized as the 'Woman Pioneer of the Year' at the ETPrime Women Leadership Awards, held in Mumbai. This prestigious award, presented by Rekha Menon, the former chairperson of Accenture India, celebrates Dr Thomas's trailblazing achievements as a woman leader in the field of science and technology, and her role as an inspiration to many aspiring women leaders across the country.

Through her work, Dr Tessy Thomas not only advanced India's missile technology but also embodied the values and vision that were imparted by Dr Kalam. Her career is a testament to the power of inspired leadership, dedication to mission, and the belief that technological advancements can be harnessed for the greater good of maintaining peace and security. For her outstanding achievements, particularly with the successful development and testing of the Agni-IV missile, Dr Tessy Thomas has been affectionately dubbed as *Agniputri* (daughter of fire). This title reflects her significant contributions to India's missile technology and her leadership in a field that has been traditionally dominated by men.

When asked about her role in the male-dominated world of missiles, Dr Thomas famously responded, "Science has no gender." This statement encapsulates her belief that scientific pursuits and excellence transcend gender boundaries. It emphasizes that dedication, talent, and intellect are the true determinants of success in any scientific field, regardless of whether one is male or female. At a public event, she said, "A woman has to be self-empathetic, self-esteemed, fully committed, and aware of situations, along with her technical know-how and leadership qualities. Then she can be an empowered person".

Dr Tessy Thomas became a source of inspiration for many women in the field of science and missiles. While she started off as the first woman scientist in this field, the trends only got stronger for future women scientists. The world of science has never been the same after the 'Missile Women of India' left a strong mark in the field for generations to follow.

Table of Abbreviations

BSI	Botanical Survey of India
CFD	Computational Fluid Dynamics
CGSI	Consumer Guidance Society of India
CSIR	Council of Scientific & Industrial Research
DRDL	Defence Research and Development Laboratory
DRDO	Defence Research and Development Organization
ECE	Electrical Communication Engineering
IAT	Institute of Armament Technology
ICMR	Indian Council of Medical Research
IEI	Institution of Engineers-India
INAE	Indian National Academy of Engineering
ISS	International Space Station
NCAOR	National Centre for Antarctic and Ocean Research
NCL	National Chemical Laboratory
NIO	National Institute of Oceanography
NPN	Non-Protein-Nitrogen
NRIADD	National Research Institute of Ayurvedic Drug Development
PEC	Punjab Engineering College
TAS	Tata Administrative Service
TPS	Thermal Protection System
UAV	Unmanned Aerial Vehicles

Bibliography

1. 1822-1912, Dall, Caroline Wells Healey,. *The Life of Dr. Ananabai Joshee, a Kinswoman of the Pundita*. Accessed 16 Dec. 2025.
2. "The Woman behind Agni-IV Success." *The New Indian Express*, 17 Nov. 2011
3. Bharadwaj, Hareesha Rishab, et al. "Journey across the World to Study Medicine: The Anandi Joshi Story." *Journal of Medical Biography*, vol. 32, no. 4, Nov. 2024, pp. 372–79, doi:10.1177/09677720231190887.
4. Chatterjee, Asima, et al. "The Treatise on Indian Medicinal Plants." *WorldCat.Org*
5. Chawla, and Kalpana. "Computation of Dynamics and Control of Unsteady Vortical Flows." *Ph.D. Thesis*. Accessed 16 Dec. 2025.
6. EK Janaki Ammal: The 'nomad' Flower Scientist India Forgot." *BBC News*, 14 Nov. 2022
7. Digital, ET Now. "Throwback: When Infosys Founder Narayana Murthy Was Always Broke and Owed His Wife Money." *Times Now*, 9 Feb. 2021
8. *English Releases*. https://pib.gov.in/newsite/erelcontent.aspx?relid=63872. Accessed 16 Dec. 2025.
9. Gautam, Vanya. "From Tata Group To Infosys Foundation: Looking Back At Sudha Murty's Successful Career." *Indiatimes*, 12 Feb. 2024
10. Ghosal, Shibnath. "A Tribute to Prof. Asima Chatterjee." *ARKIVOC*, vol. 2003, no. 9, Apr. 2003, doi:10.3998/ark.5550190.0004.901.
11. "In Love With Rocket Science: The Story of Tessy Thomas, India's Missile Woman." *Kerala Administrative Service Mentorship Programme*, 1 Dec. 2017
12. Indian Academy of Sciences. "Women Scientists of India: Dr. Asima Chatterjee." *Google Arts & Culture*
13. "Women Scientists of India: Dr. Asima Chatterjee." *Google Arts & Culture*
14. Jayaraj, Nandita. "Asima Chatterjee, the Scientist Who Did So Much More in a Time of Less." *The Wire*, 23 Sep. 2017
15. Kannan, Ramya. "A Glorious Yellow Bloom in Honour of Botanist E.K. Janaki Ammal." *The Hindu*, 8 Jun. 2019
16. *KCGMC-Kalpana Chawla Government Medical College, Karnal, Haryana.*
17. "Magnolia Kobus 'Janaki Ammal.'" *Royal Horticultural Society*
18. "Man's Role in Changing the Face of the Earth : William L. Thomas.
19. McNeill, Leila. "The Pioneering Female Botanist Who Sweetened a Nation and Saved a Valley." *Smithsonian Magazine*, 31 Jul. 2019
20. "This 19th Century 'Lady Doctor' Helped Usher Indian Women Into Medicine." *Smithsonian Magazine*, 24 Aug. 2017
21. ncsmgov. *Indian Women in Science & Technology*.
22. Nemichandra. "Celebrating Karnataka's Women Scientists." *Deccan Herald*, 8 Mar. 2023
23. Ordinary, Down-to-earth Woman Who Unwinds By Watching Television Serials And

Cooking. Kavitha Shanmugam Meets India's Missile Woman Tessy Thomas Is An. "'We Watched Breathlessly, Praying for Inner Strength as the Missile Took Off.'" *Telegraph India,* 29 Apr. 2012

24. PTI. "Women Need to Embrace Unique Fields to Become Empowered: Missile Woman." *Deccan Herald,* 19 Mar. 2024
25. Ramesh, Sandhya. "Karnal to Cosmos & beyond—Kalpana Chawla's Journey Is Still a Roadmap for India's Dreamers." *Theprint,* 1 Feb. 2024
26. *Remembering Rajeswari Chatterjee, IISc's First Woman Engineer – Connect with IISc.*
27. Scientists, Indian. "Google Honours Indian Chemist Asima Chatterjee on 100th Birthday." *Economic Times,* 23 Sep. 2017
28. Sci-Illustrate. "Rajeshwari Chatterjee." *Sci-Illustrate Stories,* 7 Jul. 2019
29. *NASA Technical Reports Server (NTRS),* https://ntrs.nasa.gov/search?q=kalpana%20chawla&author=Chawla,%20Kalpana. Accessed 16 Dec. 2025.
30. "Shakuntala Devi: A Human Computer." *Cuemath,* https://www.cuemath.com/learn/Shakuntala-Devi/. Accessed 16 Dec. 2025
31. Sinha, Akash. "Missile Woman Of India: Meet Senior DRDO Scientist Dr Tessy Thomas, Brain Behind Agni-5, Who Once Aspired To Become IAS." *Zee News,* 10 Jul. 2023
32. Stephanie. *ALD23: Professor Rajeshwari Chatterjee, Engineer – Ada Lovelace Day.*
33. Thanvi, Ishika. "Meet Aditi Pant & Sudipta Sengupta, 1st Indian Women To Visit Antarctica." *SheThePeople,* 23 Mar. 2024
34. *The First Indian Women Who Visited Antarctica.*
35. *The Hindu : The Nuts and Bolts of a Superachiever.* Accessed 16 Dec. 2025.
36. The Telegraph Online. "Lady Who Spoke 'Native Language' of Numbers." *Telegraph India,* 22 Apr. 2013
37. TNN. "A First: Woman to Head DRDO's Agni-II Project." *Times Of India,* 14 May 2008
38. "We Watched Breathlessly, Praying for Inner Strength as the Missile Took Off?" *The Telegraph,* Accessed 16 Dec. 2025
39. "Who Is Anandi Gopal Joshi?" *The Indian Express,* 31 Mar. 2018

Praise for the author and her works

"... priceless tips for startup expansion and management. [Ganesha's Global Startup] is a must read..."

– The Times of India

"...handpicked success mantras... [Startup Secrets from the Ramayana] must read for budding entrepreneurs."

– The Times of India

"...[Superwomen] unleashes the secret of achieving your passion... perfect combination of emotion and intelligence."

– Women's Era

"...[for] youngsters looking for inspiration, this might be the one."

– Hindustan Times

"Interesting journey of how 20 women played fantastic roles towards perfection..."

– Millennium Post

"This book encourages entrepreneurship in the youth..."

– Hindustan